Patton
on Productivity:
Proven Techniques
for Effective Management

Patton
on Productivity:
Proven Techniques
for Effective
Management

John A. Patton

Prentice-Hall Inc., Englewood Cliffs, New Jersey 07632

226053

Library of Congress Cataloging-in-Publication Data

PATTON, JOHN A. (date).
  Patton on productivity.

  Includes index.
  1. Industrial productivity 2. Industrial
management. I. Title.
HD56.P35 1987   658.3'14   86-18745
ISBN 0-13-654401-0

Editorial/production supervision and
  interior design: **Patrick Walsh**
Cover design: **Photo Plus Art**
Manufacturing buyer: **Rhett Conklin**

Portions of this book were published previously by AMACOM, a division
of American Management Associations, under the title *Patton's Complete
Guide to Productivity Improvement.*

Printed in the United States of America

10 9 8 7 6 5 4 3 2 1

ISBN 0-13-654401-0   025

Prentice-Hall International (UK) Limited, *London*
Prentice-Hall of Australia Pty. Limited, *Sydney*
Prentice-Hall Canada Inc., *Toronto*
Prentice-Hall Hispanoamericana, S.A., *Mexico*
Prentice-Hall of India Private Limited, *New Delhi*
Prentice-Hall of Japan, Inc., *Tokyo*
Prentice-Hall of Southeast Asia Pte. Ltd., *Singapore*
Editora Prentice-Hall do Brasil, Ltda., *Rio de Janeiro*

I would like to dedicate this book to my wife, Helen, for her patience, tolerance and total support in all my endeavors.

Contents

Preface

Now that I am retired and have a better opportunity to speak my mind, I have also had the opportunity to reminisce. It is very rewarding to me to have been an executive in one of America's larger corporations, as well as president of my own management consulting firm.

Much of the information contained in this volume is based on my own personal experience. In retrospect I sometimes feel I should have paid for this experience rather than being paid for it.

In my retirement, with more time on my hands, I feel it is a good opportunity to pass down to others some of the things I've learned.

I realize I've been particularly critical of management. I hope this criticism is taken in a constructive manner.

Much of what is said in this book is not to be found elsewhere and is rarely discussed for fear it might rock the boat. The techniques described in these pages are all tried and proven programs that were used by myself and my engineers with rewarding results.

In all sincerity I hope they are as helpful to the reader as they have been for me.

John A. Patton

Acknowledgments

To list all the clients, friends, and business associates whose thoughts and services over the past 35 years have contributed directly or indirectly to this volume would probably fill another book.

I am very proud of the contents of this book. It is the result of my lifelong experience in productivity improvement and cost reduction. Despite this, I am aware of my own shortcomings, one of which is that I have never been accused of being a master of the English language. I emphasize this point because the book could never have been written without the organization, rewriting, and finesse brought to it by Jack Lewis, my associate for the past 15 years.

A good part of the material in this book is taken from the actual tried and proven procedures of my management consulting firm. I am further indebted to William Oshinski who was responsible for carrying out these procedures. I also want to thank Brice Maddox for his professional critique of the entire manuscript.

Introduction

The pundits who attempt to forecast changes in our national economy and life-style are almost always wrong. Their dismal track record stems from the fact that they tend to base their predictions on the indefinite continuation of present trends.

The poet and philosopher George Santayana once observed that nations that ignore the mistakes of history are bound to repeat them. The advice seems particularly appropriate when applied to our present industrial situation.

We live in an era when society is becoming more and more polarized. For people whose Bible is the Dow-Jones average, we are on an unprecedented wave of prosperity. Yet for many people in the farm economy and in areas that were traditionally supported by labor-intensive industry, the current economic picture is grim. And it is tragedy for the tens of thousands of homeless and millions of unemployed.

The situation has America's economic experts searching frantically for some solution. Yet suggested remedies have, for the most part, consisted of attempts to duplicate therapies that have worked in the past. Apparently what few people realize is that the causes for this dilemma consist of a vastly different set of circumstances than any other crisis of this type in recent history. America, and to some extent the entire world, is now experiencing what can best be described as "the end of an era."

In many ways the situation is comparable to conditions that existed in the early years of the Industrial Revolution. Then, huge segments of the population who were engaged in producing hand-crafted commodities and family farming were suddenly displaced by factory-made consumer goods, mill-produced textiles, and mechanized agricultural methods.

Today's difficulties are startlingly similar, except that now the displacement of workers in labor-intensive industries is brought about by the use of robots, computers, and electronic technology. Not even white-collar employees are exempt. But whether the phenomenon is caused by machinery or microchips, the result is the same.

Our economy has become further bogged down by a reduced demand for the raw materials used to manufacture numerous consumer items. The energy crisis of a few years back has stimulated a trend toward smaller cars, smaller homes, and more cost-efficient household items made from materials other than traditional copper, lead, and zinc.

America's reluctance to recognize our present industrial woes as a different breed of cat is, to me, a bit frightening. Both industry and the people it employs and labor unions and the people they represent must face the fact that a sizable portion of the jobs that existed a few years back are gone forever. They will not be reincarnated if America is to remain a competitive force in the world market.

The failure of our politicians, industrialists, and union leaders to realize this is all the more bewildering in view of the mistakes that were made during the first Industrial Revolution. Historians generally agree that the Industrial Revolution in America occurred between a period shortly after our Civil War and the 1880s. The same thing happened in England between 1760 and 1820. Based on this, our nineteenth-century economists should have recognized the symptoms and avoided some of the mistakes made by our English cousins. Yet then, as now, they seemed more concerned with obsolete precedents than they were with getting to the root of the problem, *a factor that resulted in decades of misplaced industrial workers on both sides of the Atlantic.*

Few would seriously suggest that the remedy lies in refusing to accept today's labor-saving innovations. From a long-range standpoint this type of change increases productivity and will ultimately provide a better life-stlye for all concerned. This was proved during the first Industrial Revolution in both England and America. In fact, some historians have suggested that it was a major factor in the expansion of the British Empire. However, the price that must be paid for an improved life-style is initial unemployment and displacement of individuals who work at occupations that become obsolete.

Having made this statement, I can almost hear the cries of anguish from areas hit hard by mass layoffs. "How long, O Lord?" they will say, "How long?" And the answer to this altogether reasonable question is: "Until government, labor, and management recognize the problem and take some meaningful remedial action."

What can be done? In my opinion, there are numerous ways to shorten the economic hardship that lies ahead. Industry, organized labor, and government can, either unilaterally or jointly, develop programs designed to retrain workers who have the aptitude for the new job concepts.

A few projects of this type have already been started. In California, a $10 million program was set up a few years ago to retrain unemployed auto workers. It was financed by $3 million each from California and the federal government, plus $2 million each from General Motors and the United Auto Workers (UAW). Ford Motor Company and the UAW have a program for a nationwide network of similar training facilities.

Since not every production employee can be absorbed by industrial procedures whose reason for existence is to reduce the work force, there will still be a residue of surplus personnel. Many of them simply will not fit into the mold of the new technology.

We can expect, in the future, to hear loud wails from union officials and politicians seeking approval for a shorter workweek to keep these individuals employed. This will not occur unless the new technologies can upgrade productivity to a point that makes it feasible. Should it occur, a shorter workweek will result in more free time for the work force and create a greater demand for employable people in recreation and service industries.

The balance of the surplus work force must then face the probably unpleasant fact that our national economy requires that they be trained in other skills. But for these individuals the shape of things to come may not be as grim as it appears.

According to the Bureau of Labor Statistics, the U.S. economy will add nearly 16 million new jobs between 1985 and 1995. Nine out of ten of these jobs will be in service-producing industries.

Based on present trends, professions that show maximum promise for future job seekers are computer programmers and systems analysts, medical assistants, computer operators, physical therapists, and electrical and mechanical engineers. But these professions also normally require more intensive training.

Fields that can be expected to hold their own, but that require less initial preparation, include travel agents, waiters and waitresses, nursing aides, orderlies and attendants, salespersons, automotive mechanics, guards, restaurant cooks; and there are many more.

Resolving the problems generated by recent changes in technology won't be easy. Coping with radical changes seldom is. In the period since World War I, 9 million farm workers were displaced. Yet most of them went on to find better paying and more rewarding jobs in other types of work. Equating this to our present situation, who can say that a steel worker laid off by a mill closure, having once made the change, won't find work in a service-oriented industry vastly more rewarding than his former occupation?

And from the consumer's standpoint, this could be the perfect time in history to beef up some of our service industries. After all, service in recent years has all but disappeared from the American scene.

It is good to know that government, labor, and management have put the wheels in motion for training workers to help them cope with the serious job-displacement problem. However, what I have tried to emphasize is that, although the start is good, *we must multiply our efforts many times. Like it or not, we are going through a Second Industrial Revolution.*

In the meantime the business community, which is also exposed to these quantum leaps in technology, must work as never before at the challenge of updating methods and techniques if it is to keep in step with a fast-changing world.

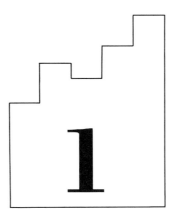

Taming
the Three-headed
Monster

The time to guard against corruption and tyranny is before they have gotten hold of us. It is better to keep the wolf out of the fold than to trust drawing his teeth and talons after he shall have entered.

Thomas Jefferson

Under the best of conditions, the process of getting a new product on the market is a long and complicated one that cuts heavily into the bottom-line profits long before the first item rolls off the assembly line. Most of the expenditures are inevitable. Things like the development of new equipment, space for construction, research and development, and dozens of other factors have been with us since the dawn of the Industrial Revolution. In the past several decades, however, the normal planning process has become even more complex.

Today the old axiom, "Let a man build a better mousetrap and the world will beat a path to his door," must of necessity be modified to read "Let an individual produce a better product and it *might* sell, providing labor unions can agree on an appropriate wage scale for the services of their members; the product will not endanger the environment; and the licensing fees, embargoes, safety regulations and other assorted red tape do not make the cost of production prohibitive."

Stated another way: The law of the marketplace must now be in conformity with the laws of federal, state, county, and municipal governments and subjected to the approval of powerful and self-serving labor unions. It must also be able to survive the pressures exerted by various self-interest groups.

Let's consider a typical new enterprise: A major automobile manufacturer wants to put a new car on the market. Space requirements at the main plant necessitate constructing a new facility in another city. Research and development has been completed, a site for the new plant has been selected, marketing experts have determined that the product has a strong potential market, and tentative financial backing has been lined up. Based on present costs and existing trends, it is estimated that the facility could be constructed for $200 million and the first car could roll off the assembly line in 18 months. The board of directors says "go." A press release is issued announcing the intention of locating the site in Anytown, U.S.A.

The company is anxious to get the product on the market in time to compete with a similar Japanese model. Within a week a group of high-ranking company officials is dispatched to Anytown to begin preparations.

They are met at the factory by a highly vocal group of local homeowners carrying placards protesting construction of the new facility near a residential area. Failing to reason with them, the officials return to their hotel in the downtown area where they are greeted by officials of the United Auto Workers union. A rumor has been floating around, they are told, that building the new model car will require closing an existing plant. Will the displaced workers have priority to work at the new plant and, if so, how will this affect the provisions of Article XVIII, Section 4, of the existing labor–management contract, which states: "Employees will not be moved more than 20 miles from their present workplace"? Also, since it is obvious that the company will be hiring considerable local labor, do they intend to pay them at a lesser rate than the wages guaranteed under Article XIX, Section 9, of the present contract? There are more questions and demands, but for the present let's leave it at this point.

The next roadblock occurs at the county commissioner's office where they are advised that Anytown, U.S.A., has historically been a residential community. Because of this, a clause was inserted in the county charter back in 1948 which stated that any heavy industry would be subject to real estate taxes at two and a half times the basic rate for residential property. Later, at the State Highway Commission, they are told that projected traffic to and from the plant will necessitate improvement of existing roads and highways. Is the company ready to assume all or a portion of these expenditures?

Somewhat frustrated, they proceed down to City Hall. They are met by the mayor and a covey of reporters from the local news media. Under a battery of klieg lights a TV anchorwoman asks, "When your company imports over a thousand outside workers and their families, what impact will this have on the local school system? It's already overcrowded. Would your company be willing to share the cost of building a new school? And where are these people going to live? Can we expect a dramatic increase in rent and real-estate costs? Some of our senior citizens can barely make it under present conditions. Would some form of subsidy for these people, to come out of company profits, be appropriate?"

The TV camera suddenly shifts and pans in on a protestor who has elbowed his way to the front of the crowd. "What do you hope to accomplish by carrying those placards?" the anchorwoman asks.

"We're in the process of requesting a government-sponsored environmental impact study," the man says. "Anytown doesn't need any smokestack industries!"

"And how long will that take?"

The protestor shrugs his shoulders. "Probably a couple of years."

"And who'll pay for this?"

"I dunno. The company, I guess."

Lee Iacocca could probably come up with a more comprehensive scenario. But no doubt he'd agree that the events are typical. All of them add up to one thing: delays and additional costs. By the time the first automobile rolls off the assembly line, if it ever does, the time span will have stretched from 18 months to at least 30 and the unit cost will have been raised from $7,500 to $10,200. The customer will be the loser. The company will also suffer, since adding the extra costs to the retail price will probably place the product in a poor competitive position with foreign imports.

HOW DID WE GET WHERE WE ARE?

Who do we blame for all this? Government? Most people in this country have at some time deplored the intrusion of government bureaucracy into their private affairs. Organized labor? Few would deny that big labor has acquired gains all out of proportion to the additional productivity it contributes. How about management itself? Can management hold itself blameless when most, or many, firms do little or nothing to alleviate counterproductive practices? Certainly there is enough blame to go around.

In previous talks and writings, I have referred to the interdependency of labor, government, and management as the three legs on a stool that has become all but unusable because the legs have become loose and wobbly through constant abuse. It has occurred to me recently, however, that because of the intensity of the problem the three-legged stool analogy may no longer be valid.

An even better comparison might be to regard this interdependency as a three-headed monster, with each of the heads containing as individual brain that is able to think independently. Now let's use our imagination a bit and say that each individual brain has its own personality. The head on the left is work oriented. The head in the middle likes to analyze and direct things. And the right head worries about what the other two heads are doing. From left to right, we will label these three heads labor, management, and government.

Because of its awesome size and strength, this three-headed monster is normally able to cope and survive quite well. But it also eats a lot, and during some dry seasons there is not enough food available to support the appetites of all three heads. When this occurs, each head begins to nibble at the adjacent heads, sometimes with disastrous results. Unfortunately for the middle head (management), it is assailed on both sides and frequently has difficulty fighting back.

If we wish to carry the analogy a bit further, we can speculate that because of frequent abuse the middle head may sometimes become weak and incapacitated. When this happens, the nutrition absorbed by the monster's outside heads (remember this is a very large animal) is no longer sufficient to meet the needs of the monster's life-support system. At this time, since the two outside heads do have some reasoning power, they are forced to cease their nibbling tactics if the body of the monster is to survive for long.

With this rather improbable image firmly fixed in mind, let's take a close look at the thinking that takes place in each of the monster's heads. First government . . . .

DO IT MY WAY OR ELSE

During a trip to Sweden the author ran into a gentleman who owned and operated a small export firm. He had spent a good deal of time in America and was extremely sold on the American way of life and high standard of living that could be enjoyed by the average citizen. His enthusiasm was so strong that eventually I was prompted to ask him what, if anything, he found wrong with America. He pondered the question for a moment and then said, "What I find amusing about Americans is that they blame all their problems on the government."

At the time I had no ready answer, nor was one required. In retrospect, however, I must conclude that, in a nation that maintains a policy of freedom of speech and of the press, government is the only entity that can be "raked over the coals" with complete impunity and thus becomes a favorite whipping boy for any and all grievances. If the press makes an inaccurate statement about General Motors, it will be brought sharply to task. Individuals and labor unions have fought and won numerous libel suits based on malicious statements. Yet, barring the recent case by General Westmoreland against the Columbia Broadcasting System, which despite the platitudes issued by the plaintiff must be considered lost, no public figure in the government bureaucracy has ever addressed in our nation's courts an alleged wrongdoing.

All of which is not to say that many of the complaints about big government are not valid. A partial list of the government's ineptitude and sheer stupidity would fill a hundred volumes. Federal, state, and local governments now employ nearly 18 million people. This adds up to about one in every six in the total work force. Practically all of these people produce no tangible commodity that adds to our gross national product; yet they must be supported out of revenue derived from some form of taxation.

I can't and won't subscribe to the often-stated premise that all government workers are a "bunch of drones." A lot of the services provided by government agencies are needed. Furthermore, many government employees are hard-working and dedicated individuals who are doing the best they can within an imperfect system.

An example of the way government agencies expand can be observed at the U.S. Government Printing Office (GPO), presently the largest industrial employer in our nation's capital. The agency evolved from an almost forgotten act of Congress based on what in 1860 appeared to be a wholly legitimate need—to produce printing and binding for Congress, the Executive and Judicial departments, and the Court of Claims. It was staffed by 350 employees. From these small beginnings the GPO now, for the record, shows 6,000 employees on the payroll.

Based on population increase, it could be argued that considerable expansion was to be expected. However, the government-released figures give a distorted view of the agency's size and scope. The facts are that only 28 percent of the material ground out by the agency is printed at the government-owned facility. The other 72 percent is contracted out to private firms. Because of this, the employment figures cited by the government become purely fictional.

What does the GPO produce today? In addition to the *Federal Register*, the *Congressional Record*, and the *Commerce Business Daily*, the GPO is in the business of publishing literally thousands of books, pamphlets, folders, microfilms, and circulars, many of which compete with similar items produced by the private business community.

A total of 21,000 titles are available to the public. Subject matter includes titles like "Stimulating Baby Senses," "Heating with Wood," "Growing Chrysanthemums in the Home Garden," and

"Marine Fishes of the North Pacific." A king-sized flap has recently arisen over whether or not the publication and sale of these materials is in unfair competition with the private sector. Following the revelation that there were 850 million copies of books, circulars, and pamphlets on hand (or enough to provide every American household with 10 copies), a program was ordered by the Reagan administration to consolidate or eliminate the more unnecessary items. Some 2,000 pamphlets and periodicals were eliminated under this program. But in the meantime the printing presses were cranked up for 1,000 *new* publications.

In an effort to get an accurate appraisal of the situation, an interview was arranged for with Danford Sawyer, the U.S. Printer and head of the Government Printing Office. Sawyer, in a remarkably candid manner, agreed that the GPO is not being run efficiently. Many items have a very low sales volume, and in the last three recorded years the sales program run by the Superintendent of Documents lost $20 million.

Sawyer pointed out that, following the administration's order to cut costs, he issued instructions to furlough some government employees. That order was countermanded by the Joint Committee on Printing, and in May 1982, the U.S. District Court upheld the committee's action.

THE HIGH COST OF GOVERNMENT REGULATIONS

The Occupational Safety and Health Administration (OSHA) has issued over 4,000 new regulations since 1971, many of which are ambiguous and confusing, even to OSHA officials. The bureaucracy got so bad a few years back that some of the more controversial items, likes the use of U-type toilet seats and the height at which fire extinguishers must be mounted, were eliminated. Despite this, horror stories continue to crop up. An extreme example involves an Associated Press story, later reprinted by Howard Ruff in a pamphlet titled "Free the Eagle." While working in a sewer excavation, a slab of heavy clay collapsed on a carpenter, burying him to the waist. Fireman rushed to the scene and used available construction timbers to shore up the excavation. For three hours they dug with hand trowels to release the man. The reward for their efforts was two separate citations from the local OSHA office. One said the firemen violated regulations by going into a trench more than five feet deep without the walls being supported by metal-to-metal screwjack shorings. The other charged that the rescuers didn't have advance excavation training.

OSHA is only one of some 60 government agencies whose sole purpose often appears to be little more than to swamp the executive in a quagmire of restrictions and paper work. In a syndicated column by Jack Anderson, published in 1982, it is reported that American business must prepare an estimated 114 million forms of 15,000 different types for the federal government alone. Additional forms and paper work are generated by state, county, and municipal governments. Government at all levels presently consumes 40 percent of the gross national product. Fifty years ago that figure stood at 10 percent.

In the face of statistics like these, hardly anyone could blame the business community for being disturbed at government's excessive intrusions. The question, it appears to me, is "Why haven't businesspeople protested even more vigorously?" And the only answer I can come up with is "Because the businessperson generally responds by grumbling a bit, clucking his tongue a few times, and then passing the increased cost down to the consumer."

The last comprehensive survey on this important topic was conducted for *Appliance Manufacturer Magazine* by A. N. Wecksler in 1979 (it is reasonable to assume that in the past six years these figures may have been escalated somewhat). According to Wecksler, government regulations add $2,500 to the cost of a new home, $666 to the price of a new car, $42.50 to the price of a dishwasher, $191 to the cost of a central air conditioner, and $48.70 to the price of a color TV.

Are Americans ready to pay for this seemingly excessive cost of government regulations? Let's look at the record. A question posed periodically by the Gallup poll is as follows: "In your opinion which of the following will be the biggest threat to the country in the future—big business, big labor, or big government?" Back in 1959 only 14 percent of the persons queried answered "big government." In the same survey conducted 20 years later in 1979, the people who thought big government was the major threat rose to 43 percent. In the most recent survey conducted in 1983 that figure constituted a majority of 51 percent.

It would appear from this that Americans are becoming more and more disenchanted with big government. What makes reform difficult is that most people are also motivated by what can only be described as self-interest. They want smaller government, but they have become mesmerized by the benefits that trickle back in their direction.

It is probably unfair to single out any particular group to illustrate a point. However, from my own observation, few groups have been as vocal about alleged government intrusion into their affairs as the American farmer. Yet at the moment this is being written, thousands of farmers are besieging Washington to protest cuts in government subsidies.

Time now to move on to the next head of our allegorical monster. Let us consider organized labor.

MORE PAY FOR LESS WORK

Once upon a time in a country very dissimilar to the United States of today, the people who did the work were subjected to abuses they could no longer tolerate. The conditions included sweatshop labor, starvation wages, absence of job security, unpaid sick time, and general working conditions that were conducive to accidents, disease, and even death. In an effort to make things better, they gathered together in a group and refused to work until conditions improved.

Again, of course, the analogy is purely allegorical. Yet, looking at the labor picture of 50 years ago as compared to things as they are today, one might find it hard to believe we are talking about the same country. From the humble beginnings of the early-day labor movement, we have shifted to a point where compensation based on increased productivity is a myth. Almost every industry is replete with the practice of featherbedding and work slowdowns—from carpenters who will not install prehung doors, painters who limit the size of paint brushes and rollers, electricians who require skilled workers to install a light bulb, and other occupational scams too numerous to mention. The diesel engine was with us for nearly half a century before the Brotherhood of Locomotive Firemen agreed to eliminate the job of fireman. Then, of course, it was only on the basis of attrition.

In the meantime, there is a faint glimmer of light on the industrial horizon. Within the past year or so, the ravenous head of labor may have been recognizing, to a small extent, that by attempting to chew off the middle head of its own body it may be jeopardizing the chances of its own survival. For instance, in the airline and auto industries a few of the labor organizations have incredibly agreed to work for wages that are more in line with company income and productivity standards. Union membership is declining somewhat in a number of industries, indicating that even the membership has recognized that the pendulum may have swung too far. Whether or not this is a temporary phenomenon is in the realm of conjecture. I may be unduly pessimistic, but I am inclined to think that, should the monster's middle head (management) recover from its recent wounds, the left head (labor) may resume biting the head that feeds it.

CAN MANAGEMENT CONTROL ITS OWN DESTINY?

So far we have painted a rather dreadful picture of this three-headed monster. The two outside heads have been biting unmercifully on the middle head—poor management, assailed on both sides, bruised, battered, bleeding, and barely able to nurse its wounds. Were it possible to feel sorry for any portion of a three-headed monster, we would have to look at its middle head and conclude . . . poor management. And this would about sum it up. *Poor* management indeed. And wasn't this what caused most of the problems in the first place?

Can management really heap all blame for our industrial ills on the greedy labor unions or big bad government? Can it hold itself blameless when it spouts rhetoric against government intervention but becomes a warm and cozy partner when it comes to matters like government subsidies, tax loopholes, and regulations that discourage competition? Can management complain so bitterly about union encroachment on its prerogatives when it does little to provide workers with the same benefits obtained by organized labor until union organizers are camping on its doorstep?

Fully realizing that most of the people who will read this book are men and women from management, I feel compelled to make the following statement: "Most of management's problems can be identified by taking a long, hard look into a full-length mirror." What exactly was management doing while organized labor was taking over the store except to maintain a conspiracy of silence and hope that this "upstart group" would go away? Has management, for the most part, ever tried to create a climate in which employees could take their problems to supervisors instead of the shop steward? One thing is certain. Organized labor isn't going to go away. Why should it? Its practices have met with enormous success.

And how about supervision? Thirty years ago the foreman had authority to hire, fire, promote, and transfer employees. Today's supervisors do not, for the most part, even consider themselves part of management. Their authority has been usurped by the shop steward, and many supervisors take home less pay than their highest-paid production workers. Many of them have become paper-shuffling figureheads instead of leaders. Yet the irrefutable fact is that the supervisor is still the only management person who has day-to-day contact with the people who perform the work. Most supervisors today were promoted to their position on a basis of seniority or because they were the best production workers. Is it possible to conceive of a more counterproductive system? What it boils down to is that all too often the company loses a good worker and gains a poor supervisor.*

In Chapter Four, I will be discussing in detail ways and means of upgrading the effectiveness of supervision. I will outline some training programs that were successfully used in specific companies and show the results that were achieved.

Let's take another area where management has been remiss. Does anyone care about accountability anymore? Sixty percent of manufacturing companies today lack any formalized standards of accountability. This problem becomes increasingly acute when we get into the higher layers of management itself. Often there are work standards for $5 an hour production workers, but the $70,000 a year sales manager or shift superintendent is free to ignore his or her shortcomings or blame them on the computer. In Chapter Five, I will present a program by which accountability can be achieved for everyone from the janitor to the company president.

Personally conducted studies indicate that work measurement, accompanied by incentives, can raise a company's productivity over 50 percent. Studies made by others confirm this figure. Yet only 30 percent of our manufacturing companies employ wage incentives. Why aren't all companies availing themselves of this bonus? In

---

*Throughout this book, supervisor is used in place of the designation foreman, a term no longer applicable considering the large number of women in supervisory positions.

Chapter Two, I will show you how to set up a viable incentive plan that works for both direct and indirect labor, whether unionized or not.

Advertising adds heavily to the cost of today's commodities, and the cost must be passed down to the consumer. Would you like to get better advertising coverage than you now receive at a fraction of the price? I will show you how in Chapter Nine.

The basic purpose of this volume is to prove that the continuing escalation of retail costs caused by runaway manufacturing expenses is not inevitable. It is caused by management's reluctance to avail itself of a wide variety of readily available tools and techniques. When this statement was made to a business associate recently, he countered by saying that a certain amount of increased costs would always develop over a period of time. He challenged me to name a single product or service that hasn't gone up in price over 1,000 percent in the past 50 years.

I can give you an example, I told him. And it is a product you use every day. It is the service offered by your telephone company. In 1935, basic service for a single telephone cost me $5.21 a month. Now, 50 years later, I can get the same service for $6.45.

Ma Bell proved it could be done. Unfortunately, she was rewarded for her competence by having the government break up the company. In my opinion, the government should have instead asked Ma Bell to take over a few of its own agencies.

Wage Incentives
What's Right,
What's Wrong

The only safeguard of order and discipline in the modern world is a standardized worker with interchangeable parts. That would solve the entire problem of management.

Jean Giraudoux
The Madwoman of Chaillot*

Wage incentive plans are not new. Rewards have always been used to stimulate workers into increasing output. In the management-oriented society of the 1920s and 1930s, implementation of an incentive plan was relatively easy. Since there was no minimum wage, the piecework plan fixed the labor cost with no labor variance. Stated another way, management set the standards and the workers either attained them or were replaced by someone who would.

Today, before an incentive plan can be adopted or even revised, complex surveys must be taken, workable standards must be established, and procedures to be followed must be spelled out clearly and in detail. Finally, the entire package must be whipped into suitable shape to make it financially acceptable to management, but with enough earnings potential for employees, whether unionized or not, to motivate them to exert extra effort.

Various methods have been used to circumvent all the hard work and cost necessary to accomplish this properly, including outright distortion of facts, hastily constructed standards that fell apart under the weight of unforeseen problems, and complex formulas that were unintelligible to the people who had to use them.

Based on my experience, rather than wheeling and dealing at the bargaining table, more can be accomplished by a completely straightforward approach designed to sell workers or their union representatives on the altogether reasonable premise that higher pay can best be earned by the simple expedient of producing more goods in the same period of time.

The principle of wage incentives has been one of management's best tools. It has been instrumental in giving us one of the highest standards of living in the world. Yet, incredibly enough, only 30 percent or less of today's management is presently utilizing this extremely viable concept.

The sad fact of the matter is that in the United States today too few employers are taking advantage of the techniques of measured standards or incentives. Just giving a supervisor a yardstick by which to increase the performance of employees can result in a 25 percent improvement in productivity. Surveys further indicate that incentives can easily increase the gain to 40 to 50 percent.

There's not an industrial engineer or seasoned manufacturing

*Chapter Opening Quote, from "The Madwoman of Chaillot," reprinted with permission of International Creative Management (att: Bridget Aschenberg) 40 W. 57th Street, New York, NY.

person anywhere today who doesn't agree that productivity on unmeasured day work will net only a maximum of 60 percent of a day's work. When standards of accountability are used, productivity normally escalates to 80 or 85 percent. In other words, productivity can be doubled by going from no measurement to incentives.

It is most disturbing that, despite all this, incentives in recent years seem to have fallen into disrepute.

WHY THE LACK OF ACCEPTANCE

If incentives are as good as described, why are less than 30 percent of American companies utilizing this valuable tool? In attempting to respond to this seemingly simple question, we usually come up with some complex answers. For openers, there's the fact that many members of top management do not regard the wage incentive principle as the greatest thing to come along since the invention of the wheel. Their lack of enthusiasm, in many instances, seems to be based on reports from other companies where the concept has failed. Often totally ignored, however, is the fact that most unsuccessful incentive plans fail because they were not properly installed in the first place.

Critics of incentives are fond of pointing out the various problems that are often encountered when wage incentives are introduced into an organization. Cited, for example, is the possibility that they can result in higher administrative costs, increased pressure from labor groups, and discontent from some employees who may feel they are not getting a large enough slice of the pie.

There's no denying that wage incentives *are* often accompanied by problems. But since the system appears to work better from a productivity standpoint than any alternative, the difficulties can be compared, in a sense, to the problem experienced by a lottery winner who is confronted with paying income tax on the proceeds: *it's a nice sort of problem.* In fact, if properly designed and effectively administered, the wage incentive principle could well be one of the few concepts in our economic structure where everyone wins and nobody loses!

We can talk ourselves blue in the face about motivation, quality of work, and employee loyalty, and these things *are* important. But in the final analysis there is one basic factor that will inspire good productivity better than anything else. *That ingredient is money!*

All the stereotyped pep talks and management platitudes that ever came out of an industrial-relations textbook are not going to stimulate much adrenaline in the veins of an employee who's worried about where next month's car payment is coming from. Yet show him or her how they can earn the needed money in the same amount of hours and you're getting into a principle of economics with which the worker can instantly empathize.

It may be an oversimplification to say that one of the chief deterrents to the implementation of a successful wage incentive program is the fact that it is continually under pressure from all segments of an organization.

Let's face it. The best incentive plan ever devised is a fragile mechanism. All too frequently it is viewed with suspicion by the workers, treated as a bargaining chip by the unions, regarded with thinly veiled contempt by many first-line supervisors, and often considered an administrative monstrosity by some members of management. Even the industrial engineer, who is supposed to be the motivating force behind the project, is sometimes guilty of using the plan to upgrade his or her status in the organization, rather than to upgrade the effectiveness of the work force.

In view of this concentrated barrage from all directions, is it any wonder why many wage incentive plans fold up under the pressure of the first few major skirmishes?

WHY INCENTIVE PLANS FAIL

Incentive plans seldom die of natural causes but rather from malnutrition, neglect, fatal abuse, and abandonment. Almost everything that occurs to affect an incentive plan in the normal course of events is going to be detrimental. From my own experience, there are three overriding reasons that account for over 70 percent of all wage incentive failures.

The first and major cause of wage incentive failures is "average earnings." Average earnings will ultimately destroy the foundation of an incentive program. If this statement seems strong, let me go a step further and say that, after participating in numerous revisions of incentive programs over the years, I can predict that the application of "average earnings" or "guaranteed wage" invariably will result in one of the following:

1. Deterioration of incentive pace but maintenance of incentive earnings.
2. Transfer of the incentive take-home to base pay.
3. A justification to discard the entire incentive program.
4. In the worst scenario, stimulation of runaway costs that force a company into bankruptcy.

There is no close second to "average earnings" as a weapon to torpedo an otherwise successful incentive program. When drafting the manual for your incentive program, dismiss the term "average earnings" from your vocabulary.

The second reason for deterioration of many incentive plans is that individuals with operating backgrounds are not adequately represented in the higher management echelons. The May 16, 1976, issue of *Forbes* magazine described this phenomenon most eloquently. It was in an article showing the salaries of 822 chief executives together with their backgrounds. According to the article, only 10 percent of those individuals had backgrounds in operations.

Most operating executives have developed a keen appreciation of the fact that wage incentive plans can increase output dramatically with correspondingly decreased cost. Is it asking too much to expect people with backgrounds in marketing, finance, law, and so on, to be sensitive to problems that are found to bring about incentive failures, such as poor standards, inadequate maintenance, and ineffective training of supervisors? These critical problems, which have such a strong influence on the productivity of the entire organization, simply do not surface or come under discussion at the uppermost levels in many companies.

The third major cause of incentive failures is directly related to management's lack of appreciation of the supervisor's all-important place in the wage incentive program. Management does not seem to be aware that there is a definite relationship between the continued success of an incentive program and the supervisor's role in the program's day-to-day operation. This includes the supervisor's part in program development, his or her training in incentive fundamentals, and last, but most important, the degree to which the supervisor is convinced of his or her responsibility to maintain the incentives at the local work area.

DESIGNING A BETTER INCENTIVE PLAN

The formula used to determine incentive pay standards should be fair and equitable for both the worker and the employer. Ideally, the plan should perform two basic functions. It should offer the worker a greater take-home pay for improved productivity, and provide management with a larger profit because of this.

To accomplish this, both management and labor must participate in the program in an atmosphere of mutual cooperation and good faith. Nothing can impede the effectiveness of a wage incentive plan quite as quickly as allowing it to deteriorate into a one-sided instrument for either the company or the employee, unionized or not.

If a company is organized, negotiation with the union is mandatory prior to moving ahead with the plan. The first step should be for management to prepare a brief for the negotiating team. The brief should contain information concerning the management viewpoint and should attempt to anticipate questions that will be raised by employees or their representatives.

Some questions that must be considered or anticipated follow:

From The Company Viewpoint

What are unit costs at present?

What will they be after implementation?

What will it cost to implement the plan?

How permanent is the plan?

How many employees will earn more?

How many employees will have to work harder?

What problems are involved in the changeover?

What will be the economic benefit in the way of cost reduction or cost avoidance?

Is the investment economically feasible?

From The Employee And/Or Union Viewpoint

Will gains already acquired be lost?

How much more will employees take home?

Will increased effort be required to earn the same pay?

Will safeguards be given in writing?

Will the union participate in establishing standards?

Will employees be pleased or displeased?

The actual procedures to be used when installing a wage incentive plan must, of necessity, vary greatly with financial conditions, employee attitudes, and union cooperation. Great care should be exercised in the drafting and preparation of contract clauses. Once agreed upon, the details of the plan should be written in simple, easy to understand English; and once implemented, the plan must be monitored continuously for problem areas that may require revision or modification.

Prior to implementation, both supervisors and union stewards should be trained in the method by which incentives are installed, how a day's work is established, proper timekeeping procedures, and the like. Additionally, for the plan to survive long, all parties involved (management, industrial engineering, labor unions, first-line supervision, and workers) must recognize the problems as they actually exist. This is extremely important. So important, in fact, that each of these five entities should be aware of the problems and attitudes that exist in each of the five groups. Let's begin with the problems and attitudes faced by management.

Management

As the prime motivating force of any organization, top management should be among the staunchest champions of any program that has a clear effect on company earnings. Unfortunately, in the case of wage incentives this is not always so.

All too often, once they have approved the installation of an incentive plan and appropriated what they consider to be an adequate budget, top management simply doesn't want to get involved. Apparently they expect the plan and everyone connected with it to operate in the same manner as the people in the "Peanuts" comic strip, where the characters involved are able to function for an indefinite length of time without apparent supervision or control.

Sometimes this is calculated. Many top-management people prefer to remain detached so that they can play both sides of the fence as need or expedience arises. The rank and file are quick to sense this, and begin to regard the plan as something unimportant, with no serious rules, from which they are free to acquire all possible immediate gain.

With options left open, the operating manager is often in a position to bend and abuse the plan as expedience dictates. The manager can loosen incentive rates instead of raising base rates or negotiate average earnings rather than correct the causes of lost incentive earnings. He or she sometimes finds it easier to bend the rules than to insist on compliance with established controls. In short, it is much easier to make incentive concessions rather than get to the root of the problems and correct them.

In addition to plain and simple lack of interest, management is also frequently guilty of lack of backbone. When times are good, demands by the union to "water down" incentives are not challenged or subjected to serious negotiation. Instead management adopts a "don't make waves" attitude. They rationalize this with the thinking that "We're making too much money to take a strike or slowdown." As a result, management rights are eroded, average hourly earnings are accepted, excessive off-standard work is allowed, downtime is allowed to climb out of control, and earnings are out of reach. Having failed to stand up for its rights in the first place, management then finds it has very little left to stand up for.

Finally, there is the opposite counterpart to the unyielding executive who jealously guards her or his own prerogatives. This is the newcomer who is not familiar with the big picture and doesn't wish to take the time to see it from the beginning. This usually happens in larger, multiunit companies where there is often a constant turnover of middle and top management. When an incentive system is first installed in these facilities, unit costs usually go down, which more than offsets the installation, maintenance, and clerical cost, resulting in a gain for the company. However, after a few changes in management, this overall gain is forgotten, and the fixed costs of maintaining the system are questioned. Often personnel are then cut, those who are left cannot keep the standards up to date, and soon the system is out of control.

Industrial Engineer

The industrial engineer, as a major component in today's business structure, is in a unique and often precarious position. From the moment the engineer is hired, he or she is viewed with mistrust by the workers, accorded only superficial cooperation by the supervisors, and frequently treated with open hostility by the union. Even top management, who authorized the engineer being there in the first place, frequently adopts a grudging "wait and see" attitude toward his or her activities.

Even after a plan is installed, the industrial engineer is often under pressure from managers to be "practical" in solving problems and resolving difficulties. Being practical can almost always be interpreted to mean loosening standards in such a manner that the incentive levels are easier to reach. With all these forces working against the engineer it doesn't take a degree in advanced psychology to realize that to function with even minimum effectiveness the industrial engineer must first concentrate on selling himself.

If there is any single ingredient that should be part of the basic makeup of each and every industrial engineer, it should be a complete and comprehensive grasp on the working principles of good public relations. This is not always the case, and many well-designed and potentially workable incentive plans barely get off the ground, flounder briefly, and then die from simple lack of enthusiasm.

To complicate the issue still further, many managements jump over dollars to save nickels by hiring a bargain basement engineer. The industrial engineering department then becomes merely a stop-over in the training program for new engineers and partially trained people promoted from the ranks. Often these people, in their zeal to make points with top management, trade expediency for good will by cracking down on high earnings, but do nothing about low earnings, fail to keep standards up to date, and try to tell supervision what to do instead of soliciting its opinions. It then becomes apparent that the people who should be managing the program are spending more time advancing themselves than they are promoting the interest of the company.

A typical situation of this type occurred while making a survey for a large Midwest furniture manufacturer. In the course of an interview with the plant manager, he complained that the industrial engineers, both of whom had MBAs, never seemed to get anything done. He was convinced that he had done everything in his power to motivate them and had assured them that any necessary monies would be spent as long as they could be justified and met the company's payback requirements. In similar interviews with the IEs, they expressed feelings of frustration at not having the authority to get things done. The problem was obviously either a communication breakdown or an inability on the part of these two men to understand the role of staff organizations within a company.

Still another area where many IEs manage to sabotage an otherwise good wage incentive plan is in the matter of basic communication with the workers and supervisors. Terms like "input stimulation," "cost ratio," and "shared commitment" may be quite acceptable over a round of drinks with fellow engineers. But to the workers whose earnings are affected, they often are interpreted as a management snow job.

To illustrate, here's an actual incentive formula for a shear operator in a Chicago steel mill: $1.2 \times S \times RRb = Ab \times R6$. After being presented figures like this, is it any wonder that the average production worker views an incentive program with something less than wild enthusiasm?

Supervisor

In an era when it is fashionable to downgrade the role of the supervisor, it is perhaps understandable that, in their eagerness to set up an operation acceptable to both the workers and the unions, management often tends to forget to consult with the first-line supervisor. This is unfortunate. Without the support of on-the-spot supervision, the best incentive plan in the world will eventually deteriorate into a meaningless mass of figures and statistics.

Whenever a wage incentive plan is established, it is very important that supervisors in the immediate work area have a hand in the planning and formulation of the basic standards. The first-line supervisor is the integral key to good standards maintenance. In fact, they cannot be maintained unless the supervisor knows and appreciates his or her responsibilities. The supervisor is in a position to note changes in methods, tools, equipment, supplies, specifications, or quality levels. The supervisor's cooperation and good will are essential if he or she is to be depended upon to alert the industrial engineering department so that adjustments can be made.

Supervisors in some organizations become less than cooperative because of the manner in which supervisory performance is measured. Often the supervisor can profit from loose standards, if for no other reason than the fact that they mean higher earnings for the worker and therefore a happier work force with fewer problems. Loose standards can also result in a higher performance rate against standard, which is the measure of supervisory efficiency in many companies.

But more frequently the lack of supervisory enthusiasm can be traced to more subtle forces. Much of it is based on the undeniable fact that many supervisors rise through the ranks. The supervisor may have been chosen because she or he was a good worker or the senior person on the job (both, incidentally, are poor leadership criteria). Often, when this happens, even though the supervisor has assumed the mantle of leadership, she or he still frequently feels a strong rapport with former co-workers. This "be a good Joe" attitude is further intensified by the fact that the supervisor feels (many times with some justification) a lack of proper backing from top management. Hence, the supervisor becomes a person of dubious loyalties and often gives only superficial support to a program that the supervisor believes to be something ramrodded through without her or his consultation or recommendations.

In our experience, supervisors have not been given, nor have they assumed, the responsibility of preparing subordinate employees for greater responsibility. This lack of preparedness on a number of occasions has led to hasty selection of supervisors, and occasionally, without the full understanding or concurrence of the incumbent. A greater effort must be made to identify, orient, and provide initial preparation of logical candidates for supervisory positions. An important step forward in this critical area is the comprehensive program called Supervisory Inventory Analysis (SIA), which I developed several years ago. Details of this plan are outlined in Chapter Four.

Labor Unions

It is probably an oversimplification, but reduced to its simplest form the basic aim of many labor unions sometimes appears to be to get as much money for as little work as possible. Conversely, some executives, sad to state, still operate on the premise that it should be the first priority of management to get as much production for as little money as possible, with no regard for the welfare and basic needs of the people who produce the product or service. (It's encouraging to find that many progressive management and unions appear to be getting away from this frame of mind.)

With these two attitudes frequently in a head-on collision course, is it any wonder that in many companies any proposal by management to modify wages or working conditions is viewed with open skepticism by union officials? Is it any great surprise that management members often build a wall around themselves each time they talk with an officer from the union? I still maintain enough faith in the principles of free enterprise and collective bargaining to hold the unqualified opinion that *it doesn't have to be this way.*

When Cudahy Packing Company, one of the nation's largest and oldest meat-packing firms, was faced with closing its plant because of operating losses, we were retained to do what was necessary to put the organization back in a solvent condition. Oddly enough, the workers were already on an incentive plan, but the standards were obsolete and the union was adamant concerning any cut in the existing wage scale. We spent some time with union officials and managed to convince them that we were truly operating in good faith.

We then made a report of the problems together with suggested solutions and presented them to the membership. As a result, the union agreed to a revision of the incentive rates in exchange for an increase in base rates. As President Richard Cudahy stated at the conclusion of the incentive revision, "We had a complete turnaround, going from the brink of bankruptcy to the highest take-home pay and lowest costs in the history of the company."

"Sure, this might work with some unions," someone may say. "But how about the hard-nosed outfit that refuses to budge?"

To which I can only reply, "It has been my experience that, when organized labor is kept informed and allowed to participate in the program, cooperation can be expected."

The Worker

If there is any single thing that characterizes successful companies, it is that they are aware that their product is only the end result of the people in their employ. Despite this, it is absolutely amazing how many wage incentive plans can be found, even in companies that pride themselves on being progressive, that contain booby-trap standards, inequitable base rates, and only a token opportunity for adequate employee earnings. The successful incentive plan must offer a worker sufficient reward to inspire increased output. To do this, long waits and chaotic scheduling must be eliminated. In addition, no ceiling should be placed on total earnings; otherwise, incentive workers will peg production.

Whenever both workers and management have a high degree of confidence in each other, a wage incentive program is off to a good start. Otherwise, it will probably be viewed with suspicion and mistrust. To acquire the necessary rapport to achieve this, it often becomes necessary to subordinate the role of the industrial engineer and apply a liberal helping of what, for lack of a better term, we may call "human engineering." Most of the difficulties encountered in any wage incentive program are human-relations problems. And human-relations problems are best solved by human relations, rather than slide-rule techniques.

This is not to suggest that, simply by establishing an incentive system based on the principles of good faith, all employees will automatically conform like the robots in a grade B science-fiction movie. Human nature being what it is, some abuses will probably occur.

It is an enigma of our system that some people who would rebel at the very thought of stealing money from the company safe consider the firm for whom they work fair game for practices like double counting, banking, count padding, and unauthorized shortcuts in prescribed methods. They rationalize their actions by regarding the wage incentive program as a form of game in which management holds all the trump cards. To even the score, they strive to create some form of counteradvantage for the opposing team.

WHY INCENTIVE PLANS SUCCEED

The long list of problem areas cited in the preceding pages may explain, to some degree, why some managements have become disenchanted with the incentive principle and have opted instead to forego the obvious benefits in return for fewer headaches and aggravation. Nevertheless, every company is, or should be, in business to make money. Make no mistake about it, a successful incentive plan is a guaranteed money maker and should be employed wherever possible if a company is serious about bottom-line profits.

Since we have discussed most of the problems that can occur at each level of the organizational structure, let me now furnish some positive material in the form of guidelines. These have been developed over the years to alleviate areas of difficulty and ensure the program's success.

1. *Get house in order.* Work flows must be balanced and the house must be orderly. A disorderly house in this context is poor equipment, shortages of materials, and other factors that keep incentive workers from earning their extra pay. Production also suffers when these problems are not corrected.

2. *Ensure equitable base rates.* Base rates must be equitable. An incentive plan cannot be used as a substitute for equitable base rates. Base rates are for a fair day's work, and incentive earnings are for incentive performance. Incentives cannot be expected to compensate for low wages.

3. *Provide adequate training.* Training sessions are a must. They should include all members of management, as well as key members of the union if the plan is developed in a union shop. This portion of the program cannot be slighted and requires intensive effort on the part of both labor and management. The sessions should be tailored to the needs of the various groups.

4. *Provide base pay for nonstandard work.* The plan must ensure that delays and nonstandard work will not detract from earned incentive, but will be paid only at the base rate. In no instance should average earnings be paid for downtime or nonstandard work.

5. *Specify quality standards.* The plan must specify that production will meet quality standards at all times and that incentive pay will be for quality production only.

6. *Develop a comprehensive policy manual.* Policies and procedures must be clearly spelled out in a manual written in simple, understandable language.

7. *Prepare documentation of standards.* Work standards must be realistic and attainable and should be expressed in terms the worker can understand. Appropriate documentation must be established so that methods are clearly spelled out. This is especially important for conducting an operations audit or investigating a rate challenge.

8. *Never place a ceiling on earnings.* There must be no ceiling on earnings opportunity. An earnings limitation, whether by design or accident, is self-defeating and leads to restricted production.

9. *Audit standards periodically.* Work standards should be audited from time to time by the industrial engineering department. No plan should be implemented without provisions for auditing production standards at regular intervals. This is management's assurance that creeping changes can be controlled.

10. *Make provision for methods changes.* The plan must incorporate language that states there will be no indiscriminate rate cutting. However, provision must be made to spell out situations where standards will be adjusted to conform with changes in methods.

11. *Standards should be nonnegotiable.* Work standards should never be negotiated to quell worker discontent or put out fires. To do so is the same as negotiating away productivity. Money is negotiable, not time.

12. *Install supervisory incentives.* Place supervisors on incentives that are simple, effective, easily understood and measured on factors they can control. Also permit the supervisors to participate in working up the program. This procedure clearly brings supervisors into the management camp because it gives them an opportunity to be in business for themselves.

13. *Develop performance guidelines.* Insist on incentive performance for incentive pay and reflect this attitude in all facets of time study, performance leveling, standards development, and standards implementation.

14. *Hire competent engineers.* Employ qualified industrial engineers, pay them as well (as opposed to as little) as possible, and give them appropriate recognition and status.

15. *Ensure that wage incentive grievances are settled within the confines of the incentive program and that expedience does not sabotage the program.*

WAGE INCENTIVE REVISIONS

No chapter on wage incentives would be complete without some reference to the revision of existing programs that have deteriorated to where they result in more problems than benefits. Plans fall apart for a variety of reasons, many of which have been discussed previously. However, one overriding factor that is seldom considered constitutes the major stumbling block when an incentive plan must be revised. This is resistance to change by employees who are covered by the program or the unions that represent them.

Thirty years ago, in the early days of my career as a consultant, I discovered that to overcome the obstacles involved in a revision of wage incentives it was imperative to gain the cooperation of the worker, organized or unorganized. As a result of this decision, I established a firm policy regarding unions. If a company was organized, I insisted that management allow me to meet with the union leadership prior to accepting a wage revision assignment or even going into the plant.

Both my firm and I at that point were regarded as prolabor for taking this stand. However, I knew that if we did not get the cooperation of the union there was little chance for the success of the program.

In the hope of not oversimplifying, let me state that the answer to the problem of labor cooperation in wage incentives and other factors is through two-way communications and complete sincerity. Japan has already accomplished this by action, word, and deed.

Unfortunately, in America there appears to be too much communicating about communications and too little real communicating. And nowhere is this statement more accurate than in the fragile relationship between labor and management. Both entities can come up with some extremely valid arguments to support their case. Admittedly, management has frequently been subjected to demands all out of proportion to work performed and results achieved. Conversely, many executives tend to regard the people who produce their products and services as little more than an additional piece of machinery that must be reluctantly factored into the operation at the lowest possible cost. Between these two extremes is a large segment of the business community where, often through many years of give and take, a semblance of balance has been worked out. Yet, even here, it is usually an uneasy truce marked by thinly veiled skepticism on both sides.

Do we have here a problem for which there is no real solution? I like to think not, particularly since there is tangible proof that, even though conflict cannot be altogether eliminated, vastly improved relations between the people who pay the wages and those who do the work can be achieved.

For the past 30 years I have enjoyed unprecedented cooperation from organized labor in the installation and revision of wage incentives. In addition, I have been named in many contracts, both by management and labor, as sole arbiter. This was accomplished by strict adherence to the following guidelines:

1. Our insistence on meeting with the union and gaining their acceptance before starting any program.
2. Agreement by management that representatives of the union be a part of the total program.
3. Most important—doing everything possible to demonstrate sincerity and communications throughout the entire program.

COMPUTER-ASSISTED TIME STANDARDS

At least some of the resistance by management in the past to installation of an incentive principle was understandable due to reluctance to cope with the reams of bookkeeping and paper work that would be generated by the program. Fortunately, with the ever-increasing use of computers the paper work has been significantly reduced.

Recent advances in computer technology have made possible what can best be termed the "computer generation of incentive standards." A computer-oriented incentive program can now be designed with either a mainframe or even with a personal computer.

The use of computerized time standards has the following four advantages:

1. Accuracy is greatly enhanced because of the error traps that can be built into the program.

2. Maintenance of the program is significantly simplified because standards can be developed in one-third to one-tenth of the time it takes to develop standards manually.

3. Security is heightened. Access codes prevent unauthorized personnel from getting into the data base.

4. Consistency is maintained, since the engineer or other person developing the standards has less choices to make and less options to exercise.

Since it is more economical and practical to administer an incentive program with computerized standards, we may conceivably be looking forward to a sharp increase in the firms who opt for the incentive principle. And in an era when increased competition is stimulating the use of more efficient and effective methods of operation, there are those among us who would say that a marked revival of incentives is not coming one moment too soon.

Indirect Labor
Can Be Controlled

I keep six honest serving men;
(They taught me all I knew)
Their names are What and Why and When
And How and Where and Who.

Rudyard Kipling, "The Elephant's Child"'*

In recent years huge strides have been made in the measurement and control of direct labor activities.† This has resulted in a sizable *decrease* in the number of jobs that are classified as "direct labor activities." That's the good news.

The bad news is that in the meantime "indirect labor" has been increasing all out of proportion to the savings generated by fewer direct labor activities. Furthermore, management has shown remarkably little enthusiasm for attempting to impose any meaningful controls or restraints on indirect labor costs.

Here are some sobering figures recently issued by the Bureau of Labor Statistics: In the past 12 years (1973 to 1985) direct labor such as machine operators, assemblers, and production laborers has declined by 14.2 percent. These direct labor production jobs that accounted for 21.4 percent of total employment in 1973 now represent only 15.6 percent of all employment.

Meanwhile, during this same 12-year period, indirect labor such as craft and repair workers has grown 26.4 percent; managers and professionals grew 57 percent; technical, sales, and administrative support jobs gained 38 percent; and pure service jobs (food service, cleaning, personal and protective service) added 32 percent to their ranks.

Looking down the road a bit, indirect labor (mainly white collar, service, craft, and repairs) is projected to be *over 80 percent of the work force by 1995, or four times the direct blue-collar production employment.*

Bad as these statistics are, they should not really shock anyone. What else can be expected when controls in the indirect labor area are virtually nonexistent and management tends to regard many indirect labor activities as an uncontrollable Frankenstein or simply "the cost of doing business"?

This may not be a popular viewpoint. Yet when I watch the chaotic milling around that occurs in the indirect labor areas in many organizations, I sometimes wish that I had a cattle prod to get everyone moving in the right direction.

Among those companies that attempt to employ controls on in-

---

*Chapter Opening Quote excerpted from "The Elephant's Child" in *Just So Stories,* Copyright 1907 by Rudyard Kipling. Reprinted by permission of Doubleday & Company Inc., and A P Watt Ltd. on behalf of The National Trust and Macmillan London, Ltd.

†Information contained in this chapter is reprinted from *Indirect Labor Measurement and Control* by John A. Patton. Copyright 1980 Institute of Industrial Engineers, 25 Technology Park/Atlanta, Norcross, Georgia 30092.

direct labor, a sizable percentage do so by the simple expedient of adjusting indirect labor costs at a fixed percentage of direct labor. From a practical standpoint, this is roughly analogous to basing a company's power and light bill on the number of employees on the payroll.

The indirect labor complement in many companies is also distorted by the very efficiency of controls on direct labor activities. Put another way, because of compassion, union pressure, or other factors, workers laid off from direct labor jobs may be herded in desperation to indirect labor activities with little regard for what, if anything, they are supposed to accomplish in their new assignment.

TARGET FOR COST REDUCTION

In the factory, high indirect labor skills such as maintenance, tool and die, production setup, and other comparable technically skilled job functions are often poorly utilized because of no work measurement or labor control. In the office, clerical employees are added rather indiscriminately to offset peak workloads—not on the basis of engineered standards or measured workloads. Furthermore, in many industries the indirect labor hourly wage rates are rapidly approaching or exceeding those of direct labor, yet there is a widespread disparity in productive output between the two groups.

The situation is being even further aggravated because many wage packages being developed today call for greater fringe benefits. Fringe packages run from 30 to 60 percent of the total compensation cost, depending on contractual agreements or wage and salary policies applied. In other words, an employee making $12,000 a year is actually costing the company between $15,600 and $19,200, depending on the percentage of fringe benefits applied. And if the 50 percent productivity factor is considered when measuring real output, the actual wage cost is over $31,200 per year. The magnitude of this figure and the projected indirect growth rate make it mandatory that indirect labor costs be controlled.

APPLIED MEASUREMENT

A broad range of work measurement techniques are available to control indirect labor—the chief ones being predetermined time systems, work sampling, time study, and job estimates. The applicability of the different measurement techniques can be described graphically. At one end of the spectrum is the well-defined, highly repetitive type of job similar in nature to direct labor. At the other end is the vaguely identified, long-cycle work, often involving less motion but more mental effort. An order picker or file clerk is an example of someone in a repetitive job, while positions such as a computer programmer or design engineer describe the more complex work. A detailed work study would be more practical for the repetitive jobs, while project estimates would suffice for the others.

Many indirect jobs, for example, have cycle times that range from minutes to hours and even days, depending on the type of work performed. Their methods, being less repetitive and predictable, involve more creativity and more mental processes and problem-solving ability than their direct labor counterpart.

For these basic reasons, standards of performance for indirect operations need not be as absolute or precise as those established for direct labor. They should, however, be representative of the work-load requirements and serve as a management tool for planning and controlling the individual and group work effort as well.

The key to measuring tasks in indirect labor areas is maintaining consistency in the application of the measurement technique, not in setting precise or exact standards of measurement.

MAJOR BENEFITS

The major benefits of a planned approach to an indirect labor measurement and control program are higher worker productivity, lower payroll and unit costs, and better management practices.

1. *Productivity improvements.* Questions arise in the executive chambers regarding how much can be gained by measuring the indirect labor employee, the size of the savings, and whether it is wise or practical to undertake such a program. In my experience, approximately 75 percent of the clerical, administrative, and support departments can be included in a measurement and control program. Typical areas include general office, technical, and administrative functions, warehousing, maintenance, and manufacturing services.

By developing a program for the measurement of indirect labor, cost reductions of 15 to 30 percent can be realized, and the return on investment will be paid back three to five times over. The cost of administering the program will range from 1 to 5 percent of the indirect payroll.

2. *Cost reduction.* Without appropriate work measurement and labor controls, the performance of the indirect labor worker has been identified at 50 to 60 percent of a fair day's work, or approximately one-half what it should be. However, with a program incorporating measurement and controls developed for the operation, labor performance can be increased to 75 or even 90 percent. The improvement factor in indirect labor utilization will generally represent more than a 25 percent reduction in payroll costs. At today's prices, that's not a bad investment.

3. *Management practices.* Although lower payroll cost is the principal benefit to be realized, management gets many other advantages by adopting an indirect labor control program. Such a program often involves:

- Improving the productivity climate within the organization.
- Utilizing better operating procedures and work-related methods.
- Simplifying the work content into manageable units.
- Establishing standards of performance at all levels.
- Using modern techniques of work planning and job scheduling.
- Developing appropriate management controls.
- Reemphasizing the work ethic and a sense of urgency.

All this adds up to better planning and control of indirect labor hours.

ESTABLISHING MANAGEMENT CONTROL

The necessity for establishing management operating control through appropriate work measurement can best be exemplified by Parkinson's law, "Work expands to fill the time available for completion," and its corollary, "Employees multiply at a fixed rate regardless of the quantity of work they produce." Less than one-third of industrial firms and corporate offices effectively control their indirect labor costs. However, before corrective action can be effectively applied, one fundamental concept must be considered in attempting to control the indirect labor force. That is, unless the front-line supervisor is held accountable for controlling costs, any soundly engineered and well-designed cost reduction program will become virtually worthless.

The concept that cost control begins with the supervisor, as it relates to productivity management, means that any effective system of hands-on control must incorporate accountability guidelines from the time the supervisor initially assigns work to the employees, to the time the jobs in the department are satisfactorily completed.

In addition to the concept of supervisory accountability, another essential program factor must be presented. That is, executive management must make an earnest but direct commitment regarding the intent to implement a cost reduction program. This must be a highly visible commitment in the organization and not just a passive gesture if the program is to be viable.

After the program has been fully implemented, the supervisor must be charged with the responsibility of maintaining cost control in the department, and his or her performance should be measured against predetermined accountability benchmarks.

INCREASING PRODUCTIVITY
OF THE SERVICE WORKER

Controlling the burgeoning cost trends in indirect labor payrolls and increasing the productivity of the service worker are major challenges confronting management today. Research studies of clerical and administrative employees—the largest element of the white-collar work force—indicate that unparalleled opportunities await management's initiative with regard to generating work improvements and cost reductions in the office. And what is most alarming, these opportunities for improving bottom-line results largely go unnoticed.

Employment projections by the Bureau of Labor Statistics over the next decade indicate a continuing dramatic rise in white-collar and service occupations. Three major white-collar groups (managers, professionals, and technicians) are projected to grow three to four times the modest growth projected for blue-collar labor. Administrative support workers, including clerical, will also grow modestly, but will represent 16.7 percent of total employment in 1995, compared to only 15.2 percent for direct labor, such as machine operators, assemblers, and laborers.

The structure of the economy is projected to grow fastest in business services, up 2.6 million jobs alone. Eight million more new jobs will be added in trade, medical, construction, hotels, credit agencies, and financial brokers. About nine of ten new jobs will be in service-producing industries.

The reasons for these trends are numerous—consumer demand, competition, maintaining more specialized types of customer service, and the proliferation of paper work and record-keeping requirements because of governmental regulations. However, despite this white-collar employment explosion, management has been focusing its attention primarily on improving direct labor operations in the factory. Experience indicates that companies expend around 80 percent of their productive effort to control about 20 percent of the real labor cost. The collective effort of industrial engineering and other company personnel must be more productively deployed elsewhere in the organization.

Considering that the present trend in white-collar and service-worker employment will continue, management must be concerned about the decline of corporate profits and the deterioration of company service unless appropriate corrective action is taken at all levels of the organization. The indirect labor program helps provide the answer.

BASIC APPROACH TO LABOR
CONTROL

A partial solution to this management dilemma has evolved from our research and job-related experience with the service worker. My associates and I devised a three-dimensional program to effect productivity improvement and cost control in clerical and manufacturing support operations. The principal elements of the program focus on:

- Appropriate training and indoctrination of the workforce, supervision, and management.
- Basic systems analysis of work flow, procedures, and operating improvements.
- Applied work measurement for personnel planning and operating control.

Realizing any appreciable gains in productivity improvements requires integrating these three elements with a program for management controls and labor reporting and a continuing effort at improvement. Let's look at each of these aspects of control.

1. *Program training.* Individuals selected for the project should be thoroughly trained in all facets of indirect labor measurement and control so that they can be adept in counseling supervisors and managers when necessary in developing and implementing the program.

Supervisors should be oriented in the principles of work measurement, labor controls, and the overall application of the program. They must understand the concepts and participate in the design and development of the cost avoidance program at the outset if it is to be successful. The workers should also be briefed by their supervisor in program fundamentals related to their jobs.

Managers must be indoctrinated in how the program works. A working grasp of the program mechanics is essential if managers are to be held accountable for effecting cost savings in their areas of responsibility. Most successful programs are launched through a collective team effort and a genuine commitment from middle and upper management.

2. *Work identification and basic systems analysis.* An operations analysis, which is basically a preliminary study, should be made of the facility or operation to be improved. The study determines the current rate of labor productivity and the state of operating effectiveness. It uncovers marginal areas that may require corrective action improvements even before any indirect labor program is implemented. The checklist of 20 questions (Figure 3.1) may be used as a reference base in conducting the operations analysis. It will provide a general appraisal of the facility's operating condition.

The next step is to review the major work activities performed by the employees in the department. Examples of major tasks are:

Figure 3.1. *Checklist of Twenty Questions on Productivity*

HOW PRODUCTIVE IS YOUR COMPANY?

	Yes	No
1. Are late starts, early quits, and excessive personal and coffee break times controlled effectively?	____	____
2. Is management utilizing balanced crewing conditions to improve output and reduce worker-hours?	____	____
3. Is the flexibility of employees adequate for performing other jobs within the department?	____	____
4. Are time-reporting forms and procedures designed to establish a sufficient basis for labor control?	____	____
5. Does management exercise control over idle and nonproduction time in the department?	____	____
6. Are job assignments batched or grouped to reduce delays and increase productivity?	____	____
7. Are the work methods and work station layouts currently being utilized practical and efficient?	____	____
8. Does management measure employee output against a predetermined norm?	____	____
9. Are personnel requirements correlated to measure output?	____	____
10. Are work assignments planned to offset fluctuation in materials and equipment availability?	____	____
11. Are attempts being made to minimize work duplications or overlapping of work assignments?	____	____
12. Are peaks and valleys in work load controlled to minimize the necessity of adding personnel or working overtime?	____	____
13. Does management exercise control over employee turnover in the department?	____	____
14. Are the number of job classifications and the ratio of job classes to employees excessive?	____	____
15. Is management utilizing historical data as a guide in determining staffing needs?	____	____
16. Does the supervisor investigate chronic absenteeism?	____	____
17. Do the employees receive adequate instruction and training on how to do their jobs more efficiently?	____	____

18. Do the supervisors understand their role as productivity managers in the organization?   _____ _____

19. Is the labor force adjusted to correspond with
changes in business volume?   _____ _____

20. Have there been any appreciable operational
changes introduced regarding equipment, layout, or
business forms in the past 3 to 5 years?   _____ _____

Activity	*Unit*
Process invoice	Invoice
Type document	Document
Deliver parts	Trip
Repair machine	Work order
Process shop order	Shop order

This identification of key work activities is important because they function as major indicators and are used as tools to forecast personnel requirements and to adjust levels of staffing to meet business requirements.

The analysis of these tasks provides management with a basis to simplify and methodize the work. Work improvements are very important to the program. By making basic improvements in operating procedures, equipment, and work station layout—and not just concentrating on developing work measurement applications—management will strengthen its credibility and will better enlist the workers' help to improve operations and control costs.

3. *Work measurement techniques.* Work input data derived from the major tasks performed in the department have now been accumulated and analyzed. The findings will be used in developing work measurement and determining the proper staffing levels for the department.

The appropriate measurement technique should be selected and utilized accordingly when making the indirect labor studies. Various work measurement techniques are available, of which the less complicated are generally the best because "precise" standards are not usually necessary. The cost of standards maintenance must also be considered; more precision usually means more maintenance.

The most common work measurement techniques are direct

observations, work sampling, and time study. Standard data can be developed from any of these, and more than one form of measurement can be used in the productivity program. The chief benefit of work measurement is feedback. Supervision and management are provided with accurate and timely report data highlighting worker productivity, time spent on measured work, and cost effectiveness.

When work output standards have been developed for the various activities in the department or work center, work loads should be balanced and evenly distributed among the employees where practical. The staffing requirements can now be more reliably determined, and adjustments in personnel can be made accordingly before implementing the program. This is accomplished by making a personnel analysis of the department under study. The worker load is calculated from volume data collected for a period representing approximately one month and from measurement standards developed for the key activities. (The output of the department may be expressed on a weekly basis for planning purposes.)

Here are data representing the major work activity of a typical department:

Activity: Processing invoices

Standard: 6 minutes (a.10 hour) per invoice

Units produced per week: 1,810 invoices

Hours required per week: 181 measured hours

Present staffing: 8 employees

Using these data, the proper worker load for the department can be determined as follows:

$$\text{Units produced} \times \text{unit standard} = \text{Hours required}$$
$$1810 \quad \times \quad 0.10 \quad = \quad 181$$

$$\text{Net hours available*} - \text{Hours required} = \text{Excess hours}$$
$$304 \quad - \quad 181 \quad = \quad 123$$

$$\frac{\text{Weekly excess hours}}{\text{Hours in workweek}} = \frac{\text{Equivalent excess}}{\text{employees}}$$
$$\frac{123}{40} = 3.1$$

*Calculated by subtracting estimated absenteeism, vacations, and so on, from total hours available; in this case, 320 − 16 = 304.

Staffing guides should be established at variable work input volumes to maintain proper crewing levels. These guides, or charts, show the relationship of business volume and staffing required to process the work load in the department.

The framework for constructing a staffing guide using data developed for a representative department follows:

Major volume indicator: Invoices processed

Minutes per invoice: 6(0.10 hours)

Hours available weekly per employee: 40

Units processed per worker-week: 400 (40 divided by 0.10)

The staffing guide shown in Figure 3.2, based on these data, expresses staffing requirements in increments of 0.5 employees because it enables management to work overtime to handle brief increases in volume, rather than add another employee. Temporary help can also be considered in this situation.

4. *Management control and labor reporting.* After the work measurement phase of the project is completed, labor controls should be developed. Labor controls are the principal management tools used to contain costs.

Management should install a worker utilization reporting system to monitor employee activity and evaluate individual and departmental performance. This reporting system is an integral part of

Figure 3.2. *Typical Staffing Chart*

Accounts Payable Department
Weekly Staffing Chart

Invoices Processed	Required Staffing
1–400	1.0
401–600	1.5
601–800	2.0
801–1000	2.5
1001–1200	3.0
1201–1400	3.5
1401–1600	4.0
1601–1800	4.5
1801–2000	5.0

the total program and is a useful accountability tool that extends from the worker to the supervisor and farther up to the manager. A manual of operating procedures is then prepared to assure maintenance of the program as it is installed.

Upon completion of the productivity study, management makes a preinstallation check to point out any sensitive areas of employee concern. It will identify work-flow problems that have not been improved and highlight conditions requiring corrective action before the actual installation of the program.

The major factors in making the program work as designed are numerous and revolve around the supervisor. The key actions that supervision and management must be concerned with follow:

- Determine the required staff level *before* installing the program and maintain balanced staffing in the department.
- Plan flexible work loads for assigning work to the employees. Measure progress and determine the overall work-load status in the department.
- Follow up on late assignments and take corrective action to alleviate delays.
- Use the control forms as designed and follow the operating procedures in installing the program.
- Analyze worker utilization and look for trends in input–output relationships. Monitor work-load conditions closely.
- Maintain open communications. Discuss technical and human-relations problems with the appropriate people and chart a course of corrective action.
- Plan for tomorrow when developing work assignments and maintain management control over the department.

Management should also utilize the key indicators established for each area under control as barometers to forecast the planned personnel requirements at various levels of business volume. Periodic management follow-up should be routine throughout the program's development and implementation.

Examples of the basic control forms used to measure departmental and facility performance are shown in Figures 3.3 and 3.4 later in this chapter. These forms cover a manufacturing support installation but could reflect a clerical operation as well. They show the relationship of activities performed, standards of measurement, and labor performance. The management report is the key control document used in the productivity improvement program.

5. *Improvements to the system.* Management should establish bench marks at the outset of the productivity program and document the possible improvements that were identified in the operations analysis. Key project responsibilities should be delegated and a timetable established to initiate further improvements to the program.

These bench marks function as reference points to control all activities concerning the indirect labor project. A Gantt-type activity chart is used to time-scale the job schedule and monitor planned activities in comparison to the actual events to determine project status.

Improvements to the indirect labor system can cover many facets and affect all levels of the organization. The principal improvements will come from establishing new operating procedures, adopting new business systems, utilizing better methods to process documents and related paper work, balanced staffing, and work station redesign.

PROGRAM RESULTS

The implementation of a productivity management program enables the progressive firm to reduce operating costs from 20 to 30 percent. It instills a management philosophy that costs *will* be controlled and generates a sense of urgency extending from the top of the organizational ladder down to the bottom rung.

The program recognizes the effort of the exceptional employee, as well as the contribution of the everyday worker. Furthermore, studies have proved that the morale of the work force will be improved. Management is thus provided with hands-on tools to achieve and maintain total operating control and utilize the work force more efficiently.

In a program we developed for Mars, Incorporated, we installed production standards for both direct and indirect labor. Once the program was fully implemented, Forrest Mars, chairman of the board, went on record as saying that Mars, Incorporated, achieved the highest take-home pay with the lowest bar cost in the industry. A similar program conducted at Rockwell Standard (now Rockwell International) resulted in a 28-percent increase in productivity in the year following implementation.

APPLICATION OF WORK
IMPROVEMENT PROGRAMS

The application of a work improvement program by which supervisory training, basic systems analysis, work standards, and management control are intelligently blended together results in an effective cost-control program. The program provides supervision and management with modern cost-effective tools to plan and measure work loads, improve employee productivity, and control payroll costs.

Clerical, administrative, and manufacturing support areas where work improvement programs have been effectively installed include:

- *Accounting:* accounts receivable and payable, credit and collections, and payroll.
- *General office:* purchasing, customer service, sales and billing, key punch and data processing, and other processing.
- *Office services:* stenography, typing, filing, printing, duplicating, and mail room.
- *Technical services:* drafting, engineering, cost estimating, and designing.
- *Manufacturing support services:* shipping and receiving, warehousing, and stockrooms.

MAINTENANCE OPERATIONS
ANALYSIS

Maintenance has become an increasingly important item in the budgets of most organizations. Manufacturing concerns, banks, hospitals, and retail malls are all struggling with the increasing costs of maintaining buildings and equipment, as well as with keeping their operations in smooth running order. Interruptions related to ineffective maintenance procedures and poor control of the maintenance work force are a major factor in today's operating costs. It is essential for management to recognize that maintenance costs *can* be controlled and to step up efforts to get more effective maintenance at less expense.

An in-depth operations analysis of the maintenance department will determine the feasibility of developing a comprehensive maintenance management program. A detailed operational study will highlight symptoms of excessive costs, poor planning and control, operating ineffectiveness, and lack of appropriate management reporting information. Upon completion, the study will provide management with a framework for developing a maintenance cost-control system that can be successfully tailored to company operations.

An analysis of the maintenance functions should cover these four categories.

1. *Organization.* Review and evaluate the principal functions of the maintenance department for organizational and operating effectiveness. The size of the maintenance operation should be objectively determined. It may be somewhat proportional to the number of production employees, but equipment attention, service levels, and the complexity of the facility's operation must also be considered in determining its proper size. The purpose of the maintenance organization and its reporting relationships and responsibilities must be clearly defined to prevent line and staff conflicts between maintenance and other departments.

2. *Operating effectiveness.* Analyze the cost effectiveness of the maintenance operation and look for trends in labor utilization and materials expenditures. Determine the extent that the maintenance costs are increasing by expressing this expense as a percentage of the total operating cost over a three- to five-year period.

Summarize the amount of maintenance overtime worked and ascertain whether it is excessive. Review the types and frequency of cost controls used in the operation and analyze downtime records, breakdowns, types of equipment repairs, and other factors. Determine the ratio of productive time and nonproductive time worked by craft workers and/or technicians.

Evaluate the investment in materials stores inventory and determine the availability and need for equipment replacement parts and maintenance supplies. Review the methods employed to control these materials and their replenishment and evaluate the effectiveness of the methods.

Review the general maintenance expenditures for outside services and justify these costs. Conduct work sampling studies and make a sufficient number of observations to determine present levels of productivity and labor efficiency. Determine the flexibility of maintenance craft personnel and review the present methods of in-house training.

3. *Management planning and control.* Evaluate the methods and procedures used by supervision for planning and scheduling work assignments. Look for examples of poor conformance to work schedules and job priorities. Observe the maintenance work force and determine how well the workers are being utilized on productive work. Ascertain the number of job delays due to parts and materials shortages and poor maintenance inventory planning.

Determine the size of the work loads in the department and evaluate the backlog condition. Compare this condition to overtime worked in the department. Analyze the frequency of worker-hours assigned to correct emergency work conditions, and determine the amount of time that production equipment is down. Make a random sampling of the completed work orders and note the range in time for doing comparable jobs.

4. *Management information reporting problems.* Study the types of operational reports generated from this department and evaluate the flow of management information. Determine if the computer is used effectively in accumulating historical data and reporting maintenance information. The management information reporting function should cover activities embracing labor productivity, equipment repair costs, preventive maintenance applications, materials inventory, and work loads.

MAINTENANCE PROGRAM FACTORS

As evidenced by the recent trends in maintenance costs, the need to control maintenance expenditures is more important than ever. Nine major factors to be considered in developing a viable maintenance cost-control system to improve labor productivity and reduce operating expenditures are described next. The integration of these major factors will provide an effective maintenance cost-control system.

1. *Maintenance training.* The training of maintenance craft personnel and supervisors in the latest techniques, practices, and materials is an ongoing factor if a maintenance organization is to be effective. Training strengthens an organization, motivates craft workers to upgrade their skills, and creates job satisfaction.

2. *Maintenance organization.* An efficient maintenance operation begins with effective organization. The maintenance department's functions and responsibilities must be clearly defined and its rela-

tionship to the total organization must be set out accordingly. The maintenance department must be oriented to cost control and operations.

The size and complexity of a maintenance operation will vary according to a company's requirements. Sophisticated equipment generally means that more maintenance craft specialists are required. The number of shifts operated and the location of operations are critical factors that must be considered when estimating supervisory coverage and maintenance effectiveness.

3. *Management controls.* The optimum control of maintenance expenditures requires a coordinated application of labor and materials controls. The work order and materials requisition are the key control documents in the maintenance cost-control system.

Maintenance repair operations should be covered by a work order or job ticket. Materials or parts must be requisitioned through production cribs and charged off appropriately to the project if any semblance of cost control over materials is to be maintained.

4. *Preventive maintenance.* A viable preventive maintenance program is an integral part of a balanced maintenance cost-control system. Scheduled maintenance covering systematic inspections, repairs, service, and lubrication will reduce downtime and help control maintenance costs.

A complete preventive maintenance program should also provide for planned and scheduled replacement of troublesome equipment in the coming year.

5. *Materials inventory.* Hands-on control over maintenance materials is essential to eliminate unnecessary inventory investment and reduce parts shortages. The materials requisition mentioned in item 3 provides the basis for compiling and allocating materials costs.

Materials inventory can be controlled in a number of ways depending on the degree of management involvement desired. A manual card system using minimum and maximum levels is one method; another revolves around a computerized program of materials requirements based on historical usage.

6. *Maintenance planning and scheduling.* Optimum utilization of the maintenance work force begins with planning and scheduling work assignments. Job priorities and maintenance work loads must be considered by the supervisor or work planner when this phase of the program is initiated. The realization of cost savings is a direct

result of careful planning and scheduling of maintenance worker-hours.

Using the work standards developed for the maintenance tasks, the supervisor can determine how long each job should take. The supervisor or work planner can batch the number of job tickets or maintenance requests that can be done in an eight-hour day by each craft worker.

Work assignments for each employee should be planned and generally grouped to cover an eight-hour day. This minimizes the gap between assignments and utilizes the maintenance worker more effectively. Periodic supervisory follow-up will enable the status of the work to be determined and will create a sense of urgency on the employee's part to do the job on time. Causes of delays or jobs behind schedule can also be readily determined during the follow-up process.

The basic objectives of planning and scheduling maintenance operations are:

- To plan a full day's work in advance for each craft worker so as to minimize lost time and improve labor utilization.
- To reduce backlog conditions and work loads in the maintenance department.
- To initiate better control over the maintenance labor dollar and to handle job priorities and emergency situations more effectively.
- To improve operating efficiencies.

Maintenance planning and scheduling are essential elements of an effective maintenance organization. They operate hand in hand in determining a full day's work for each maintenance worker.

7. *Applied work measurement.* The measurement standard is the basis for establishing personnel requirements, determining work loads, and scheduling maintenance activities. This tool is an important factor in establishing labor performance and crewing levels at various inputs of work volume.

Work standards can be developed for maintenance operations using a variety of techniques. Job estimates and work sampling are the two most popular methods because of the number of variables involved. Job estimates can be refined to the point where they are quite accurate by using regression analysis, which involves plotting the actual and estimated time values for each maintenance activity on a scatter diagram. Job data are synthesized into manageable time units, and realistic standard time data may be developed from the actual estimated values plotted.

Most preventive maintenance work is repetitive and can be measured; in fact, work measurement can be successfully applied to over 90 percent of the preventive maintenance labor hours expended. The two principal techniques for preventive maintenance are time study and predetermined times.

Work sampling is used to accumulate operations data covering equipment and machinery utilization, labor productivity, and types of production delays. It can also be used to develop standards.

8. *Operating methods.* An effective organization needs uniform maintenance operations. This requires establishing standardized methods, working guidelines, and operational procedures. Standard operating procedures are critical to the maintenance organization. In essence, they enable maintenance workers to do a better job if they know:

What must be done.

Where the job is located.

When the job must be done.

How long the assignment should take.

What tools are required to perform the job.

What processes or steps are involved in doing the work.

The maintenance supervisor should be certain that all policies and procedures are written and followed and that the necessary forms, paper work, and operational guidelines are available to the worker. Troubleshooting manuals are very important in this regard.

9. *Management reporting system.* Management reports serve as a barometer of operating effectiveness. They are used to report current progress and determine whether any corrective action is required. The reporting system uses the principle of management by exception and is commonly referred to as a Polaroid snapshot of an operation. That is, it will tell you what is going on in the organization—good or bad. The principal function of the management report in Figure 3.3 is to highlight those exceptions. Management can then take corrective action.

Figure 3.3. Report for Highlighting Exceptions

REA REPORTED Indirect Labor

NO.	AREA	SHIFT	STAFFING			MVI (UNITS)	BACK-LOG HOURS AVAIL	EARNED HOURS	HOURS CONTROLLED				% PERFORMANCE		
			AUTH.	ACT.	VAR.				HOURS ON MEAS	NON-MEAS HOURS	FIXED HOURS	TOTAL HOURS WORKED	% PROD	% UTIL	% PERF
10	Production Stores	1	5.5	5.9	.4	110	—	163.0	212.4	21.6	-0-	234.0	77	91	70
		2	2.0	1.9	(.1)	36	—	54.5	68.5	9.5	-0-	78.0	80	88	70
		TL	7.5	7.8	.3	146	—	217.5	280.9	31.1	-0-	312.0	72	90	70
20	Shipping	1	8.0	9.8	.3	6315	644	318.5	375.0	6.0	11.0	392.0	85	96	81
		2	—	—	—	—	—	—	—	—	—	—	—	—	—
		TL	9.5	9.8	.3	6315	644	318.5	375.0	6.0	11.0	392.0	85	96	81
30	Quality Control	1	6.0	6.3	.3	360	—	181.4	218.6	15.4	16.0	250.0	82	87	73
		2	3.5	4.0	.5	245	—	123.9	153.5	6.5	-0-	160.0	81	96	77
		TL	9.5	10.3	.8	605	—	305.3	372.1	21.9	16.0	410.0	82	91	74
40	Set-up	1	5.5	6.0	.5	42	—	170.3	238.0	-0-	-0-	238.0	72	100	72
		2	2.0	2.1	.1	14	—	58.2	63.4	14.6	4.0	82.0	92	77	71
		TL	7.5	8.1	.6	56	106	228.5	301.4	14.6	4.0	320.0	76	94	71
50	Maintenance	1	12.0	12.8	.8	145	—	287.2	390.3	120.7	-0-	511.0	74	76	56
		2	10.0	10.1	.1	151	—	301.7	366.1	30.9	8.0	405.0	82	90	74
		TL	22.0	22.9	.9	296	2580	588.9	756.4	151.6	8.0	916.0	78	83	64
60	Tool Room	1	8.0	8.4	.4	96	—	285.6	304.0	26.0	6.0	336.0	94	90	85
		2	3.0	3.6	.6	32	—	101.2	129.0	15.0	-0-	144.0	78	90	70
		TL	11.0	12.0	1.0	128	1502	386.8	433.0	41.0	6.0	480.0	89	90	81
	TOTALS		65.5	70.9	5.3	---	---	2045.5	2518.8	266.2	45.0	2830.0	81	89	72

Figure 3.4. Diagram of Management Information Flow for Maintenance Cost-control System

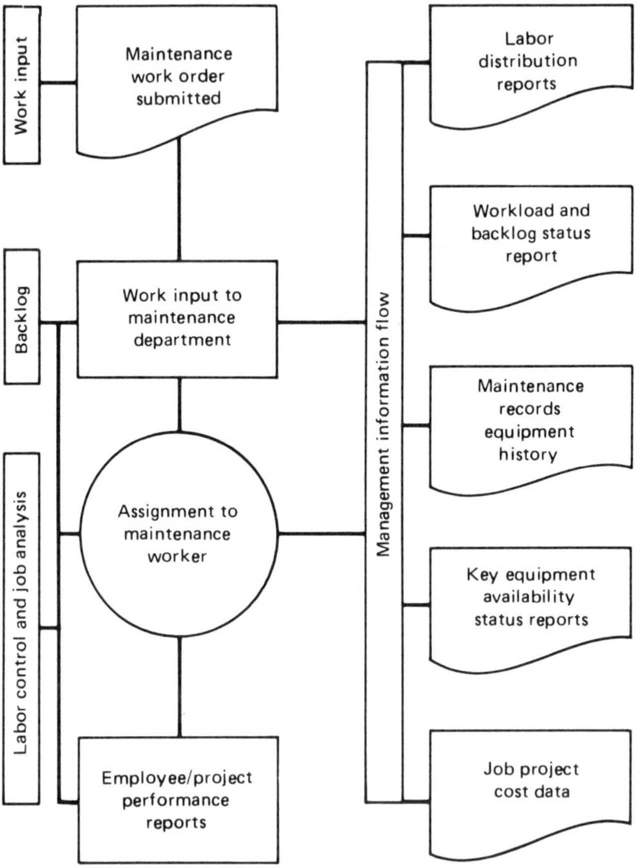

Management reports are the heart of the maintenance operation and perhaps the most significant aspect of the cost-reduction program.

A schematic diagram of the management information flow required in a maintenance cost-control system is shown in Figure 3.4. This diagram covers the control process from the time the work request is generated until completion.

CASE STUDY: CONTROL MAINTENANCE AND OTHER COSTS

The Problem: A midwestern auto parts manufacturer employing over 300 hourly workers saw its unit costs spiraling out of control and its market position threatened. The company had a sizable investment in capital equipment, but some of the manual production lines outproduced the automated ones. The key problems were production downtime, rising indirect labor costs, too much overtime, excessive absenteeism, poor work habits, and marginal employee productivity. The indirect areas targeted for productivity improvements were maintenance and tool room, materials handling, quality control, and warehousing.

Corrective Action Taken: The initial approach in correcting the problem was to make a comprehensive operational study of each of the major indirect areas so as to pinpoint the high-cost labor areas and establish a program for operating improvements. Problem analysis of the direct labor areas was an integral part of the study.

Workshops were then set up to indoctrinate the plant supervisors in program concepts and the overall approach to productivity improvements. The supervisors in turn were required to present and sell the program to the bargaining employees in their areas of responsibility. The employees were apprised that work rules would be enforced and chronic absenteeism controlled. This total commitment was necessary to accomplish the objective and get the company back on track. Workers began to feel that real job security was possible, and unit costs started to go down.

A work-order system was designed and implemented in the plant maintenance area. Supervisors now had a total management control system to assign work and to monitor employee activities, to determine backlog levels and work-load requirements, to develop priorities for critical equipment, to establish crew sizes at various volume levels, and to evaluate individual and group productivity. Preventive maintenance applications and operational procedures supplemented this program.

In other indirect areas, observations were made to establish work standards. A management reporting system was installed to monitor individual productivity and departmental activity. Labor reports were generated daily and summarized weekly.

The total program as installed was designed to assess everybody's performance, from the hourly wage earner in each department under control up through supervision to management. The accountability principle applied throughout the organization.

Results Effected: Overtime was virtually eliminated in all the plant areas. Downtime was reduced and equipment utilization went up. Indirect labor costs were slashed by a resounding 27 percent. Over $500,000 in cost savings was generated. The total indirect labor force was reduced by 23 employees, a reduction that enabled several skilled workers to be utilized in other key areas. Unit costs were improved considerably, and the company gained new leverage in the marketplace.

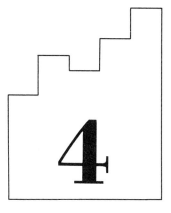

Industry's Major Problem:

The First-Line Supervisor

As I was going up the stair
I met a man who wasn't there.
He wasn't there again today.
I wish, I wish he'd go away.

Hughes Mearns*

PART ONE: SPECIFIC PROBLEMS

EARLY BACKGROUND OF TODAY'S SUPERVISOR

During the 1920s and 1930s the image of the American foreman, now referred to as "the first-line supervisor," could be roughly described as about halfway between an army drill sergeant and an all-powerful overlord. In addition to having the right to hire, fire, promote, and transfer, the foreman of an earlier era was regarded by top management as a major motivating force in the industrial structure. He was accorded a degree of prestige from both labor and management. He was responsible for ensuring that a maximum volume of work was performed in a fixed period of time. He was the source of technical knowledge, the leader of his worker group, and the administrator of discipline when needed. When he issued an order, the worker either responded or was replaced by someone who would.

From the standpoint of management and the economy of the era, it was a good policy, simple and easy to understand. And because it worked, it is perhaps understandable how management was lulled over a period of years into the belief that things would always remain that way. Unfortunately for industry, the foreman has been the victim of change, like so many other institutions. The change has been subtle and generated by a number of factors, including proliferation of staff specialists, sophisticated mechanization, automation, cost analysis, long-range planning, time studies, and numerous other management devices that tend to usurp the foreman's former prerogatives. The result is that all too often today's supervisors have been stripped of most of their previous authority and have in return been burdened with responsibility for a host of new duties they have had no part in developing.

Considering the heavy-handed approach used by many foremen of an earlier era, there may be some among us who derive a degree of satisfaction from the plight of today's first-line supervisor. Nevertheless, the occupational emasculation of this vital link between labor and management has, in many instances, all but wiped out many of the gains that have been acquired through improved techniques and better production methods.

*Chapter Opening Quote excerpted from the book *Dictionary of Quotations* by Bergen Evans. Copyright © 1968 by Bergen Evans. Reprinted by permission of Delacorte Press.

MISUSED, ABUSED, AND ACCUSED

Today's supervisors are the most misused, abused, and accused people in the organizational structure. They are overworked and underpaid, they have no real authority, and they must continually walk a tightrope between labor, management, and the trade unions. Supervisors are subject to pressures that did not exist in prewar America. They must cope with the unprecedented power wielded by labor unions, worker's rights, and a grievance procedure under which a supervisor who disciplines a worker may be called on to defend his or her action not only to the union, but to top management as well.

Labor unions recognize this. The employees they represent know it. Indeed, the supervisors themselves are acutely aware of it. The only people who seem blissfully unaware of this indisputable fact of life are the leaders of industry who pay their salaries.

Today's supervisors are weighed down on all sides by cost standards, production standards, quality standards, methods, procedures, specifications, rules, regulations, laws, contracts, and agreements. Supervisors survive in a sort of occupational twilight zone. Technically they are members of management, yet they are seldom invited to staff meetings and more often than not can identify more closely with the people they are being paid to supervise than with higher management. They are expected to work with staff specialists, the personnel department, industrial engineers, and accountants. They must know the union contract and how to settle grievances, how to cooperate with other department heads, how to instruct workers, how to maintain discipline, and how to cope with reams of paper work.

The end result is that many first-line supervisors, overwhelmed by complete frustration, develop a "what's the use" attitude and ultimately relinquish the reins of leadership to workers or shop stewards.

Obviously, under our present industrial structure it would be impractical, and indeed undesirable, to revert to the role of the authoritarian supervisor. Nevertheless, management must face up to the fact that if the present condition is to be improved, the role of the supervisor must be upgraded from that of a glorified record keeper to something resembling a symbol of leadership. Management must take the initiative in this transition. Today's supervisors are convinced that they are less, rather than more, effective; less, rather than more, important; less, rather than more, secure; and have received less, rather than more recognition.

Ironically, management has played a leading role in undermining the status of the first-line supervisor. Admittedly, staff technicians, industrial engineers, quality control specialists, and cost analysis experts are a vital part of the present industrial scene. But the supervisor is still the only direct link between the people who make policy and the people who perform the work. To downgrade the status of this individual either overtly or inadvertently is not only a contributing factor to poor productivity, but an insult to the initiative, intelligence, and morale of an important member of the management team.

Management must discard its current policy of treating the supervisor as the "little man who wasn't there." The organization that has the foresight to develop and cultivate what, for lack of a better term, I refer to as professional supervisors and pay them salaries commensurate with their abilities will reap benefits in productivity, employee morale, and increased profits many times in excess of the compensation they are required to pay for this type of expertise. To do this, management must begin by recognizing the supervisor as a member of management. Many company executives claim they already do this, but for the most part their recognition consists primarily of lip service.

During a talk I gave recently to a group of company presidents, I asked for a show of hands on the question, "How many company representatives here today consider the supervisor a member of management?"

The hands of nine-tenths of the audience went up.

"Now let me ask," I went on, "how many of you give your supervisor an increase in pay shortly after your employees' union gets an increase following settlement of a new contract?"

The same number of hands went up.

"How can you say that you regard these supervisors as members of management?" I asked. "The loyalty of these so-called members of management is tied in to your company union. They're fighting for the union to get an increase because they know perfectly well that only then will they get an increase. You gentlemen are kidding yourselves when you say you regard the supervisor as a member of management!"

Adjustments to a supervisor's pay should be established by the formulas that apply to other management positions and not be dependent on results of bargaining negotiations.

BARGAIN-BASEMENT SUPERVISION—
ITS CAUSE AND EFFECT

In a survey conducted by James E. Overbeke, a writer for *Industry Week,* supervisors were asked how they viewed their position in military terms. Were they lieutenants (meaning officers and gentlemen) or were they sergeants (meaning straw bosses)? Every one replied "Sergeants."

With an empathy gap like this existing between the supervisors and top management, it would follow that the initial step on the part of today's industrial leaders must be first to recognize the supervisor's true worth and convince them of their importance to the organization they serve. How far we are from doing this can best be illustrated by a recent advertisement that appeared in a newspaper circulated in a small American industrial city:

> WANTED: Supervisor for heavy industry assembly plant. Applicant must have the ability to work with staff specialists, personnel department, industrial engineers, and maintenance staff. Must possess the ability to lead employees and stimulate their respect. Must be knowledgeable concerning the union contract, grievance procedures, work measurement, and incentive standards. Successful applicant will also be required to instruct workers, develop more effective job procedures, maintain discipline, and process paper work generated by cost standards, production standards, quality standards, safety specifications, rules, regulations, contracts, and agreements. Salary: $16,000 a year.

Read this advertisement again. Look at the responsibilities. Then look at the salary. Does this tell us anything? It could be argued that the organization that placed this ad was only adhering to the law of the marketplace. The advertised pay, sad to state, is within the bounds of what is paid by many companies throughout the land. Moreover, there will be people who will be ready, and perhaps even eager, to take a job of this type at the indicated salary.

The advertised position will be filled. Make no mistake about that. But unless the organization doing the hiring is exceptionally lucky, it will be occupied by an individual who eventually, if not immediately, will lack credibility with subordinates, resent interference from staff specialists, have a low opinion of his or her own contribution to the organization, and harbor a marked hostility for superiors who expect work for wages that are probably lower than those received by the people supervised.

Numerous studies conducted in conjuntion with supervisor pay structure have determined that in 60 percent of the companies today skilled employees take home pay equal to, or more than, their supervisor. What is really disturbing is that when I point this out to managers in some of these companies, they say, "Well, Patton, look at the overtime these employees must put in to make that extra money."

My answer to this is "The heck with the overtime. They're taking home more *money*. It is amazing how many organizations will invest millions of dollars in high-priced machinery but flatly refuse to pay for the expertise required to ensure cost-effective operation of this expensive equipment.

OVERLAPPING LINES OF AUTHORITY

Not all the supervisor's problems are directly linked to poor pay. Part of the difficulty can be traced to low morale generated by an overlapping of authority by staff specialists who frequently usurp the supervisor's prerogatives.

The personnel director, stimulated perhaps by an ever increasing role in labor–management affairs, often either countermands or modifies a supervisor's recommendation for disciplinary action with little or no explanation.

Industrial engineers and safety specialists often arbitrarily enforce changes without prior consultation with the first-line supervisor. Cost-control people frequently lay out programs with only a superficial knowledge of the problems on the production line. The industrial impotence suffered by the supervisor as a result of these policies results in a lowering of morale and ultimately a lack of respect for the supervisor by workers, who tend to regard their immediate supervisor as an organizational nonentity with no real authority or status in the organization.

Staff personnel must be trained to channel their activities in such a manner that they work with and through the supervisors and help them increase effectiveness, instead of indulging themselves in what can only be described as a power play to control production activities.

I recall an instance that occurred when I was engaged in a plant improvement program at a southern textile mill where a departmental feud had developed between the safety officer and a supervisor whom I'll refer to as Jones. Jones was a long-time employee and a production-minded supervisor who was steeped in the premise that the supervisor in charge of a department should have complete license to ensure maximum productivity. Predictably, when the safety officer began initiating safety measures that impaired production, Jones tended to regard them with something less than enthusiasm.

His antagonism reached a boiling point one day when the safety man arbitrarily installed a series of machine guards in a low-risk area that created a bottleneck and affected the entire production line. The altercation that followed became loud and abusive. At the height of the argument the company president appeared on the scene, and both men were hastily summoned to the front office.

The president addressed the safety officer first. "What's the problem?" he asked.

"I've been hired here to ensure the safety of the workers," the safety man replied. "Yet this man resists everything I try to accomplish."

The president turned to the supervisor. "Don't you believe in safety?" he asked.

"I believe in safety as much as anyone in this plant," Jones retorted. "In 22 years of operation I've never had a lost time accident. The trouble is that our safety officer, sitting upstairs in his comfortable office, has no idea of what's needed on the production line. The necessary safety equipment was recommended and installed by me long before he came on the scene. This equipment he's putting in is unnecessary. What's worse, he doesn't even talk to me about it before it's installed."

"Do you ever discuss these matters with Mr. Jones before you implement them?" the president asked the safety officer.

"I can't talk to him!" the safety man exclaimed. "He's completely negative about any changes in the status quo."

"Would you like to receive his opinion?" the president asked.

"I'd welcome it!" the safety man retorted. "I'll readily admit Mr. Jones is more knowledgeable about his own department than I am. But so far I haven't been able to talk to him."

The problem was resolved by placing Jones as a permanent member on the safety committee, where he has since shown a marked interest in developing new and more practical safety procedures and has, in fact, contributed several valuable innovations to the safe operation of his department.

The case noted above is typical. Jones did not resent the safety measures. What he objected to was someone modifying the operation of his department without discussing the changes with him beforehand. This not only diminished his production; it also diminished his authority. And, worst of all, it diminished his pride. He had pride in his supervisory judgment, which should have been respected. Once he was given an expanded role in running the operation, he was actually able to increase his contribution to the department and to the firm.

Unfortunately, in too many instances staff specialists have been a hindrance, rather than a help to the supervisor who is trying to do a more effective job. We all fully realize that the complexity of modern operations demands specialized skills. However, all too often staff specialists tend to ignore the supervisor as a member of the management team.

Another area of conflict involves personnel representatives who often encourage employees to bring questions and problems to the personnel department, rather than encouraging them to go to the supervisor and have them handled directly by him or her. Personnel people often claim that the supervisor is not capable of handling these situations. In many instances this is only an excuse to build their own bureaucracy rather than assuming responsibility for providing the education and know-how that would permit supervisors to stand on their own. Such personnel people evaluate their own importance by the activity of the personnel department rather than by how helpful they can be in assisting the supervisor. They have, in effect, become a self-serving entity rather than functioning as a positive supportive arm to supervision—which, in the final analysis, is an important reason for their very existence.

Industrial engineers have also in many instances done their companies a disservice by minimizing the supervisor's stature in the organization. Too many industrial engineers today impose their industrial engineering methods and techniques on supervisors rather than working with and through them. A giant step in improving the relationship between the industrial engineer and the first-line supervisor would be for engineers to work hard to ensure that supervisors get credit for any and all accomplishments in their departments. Staff assistance should, of course, be made available, but the staff should not be given the authority to dictate to the supervisors.

These conditions do not exist in every organization, but they occur often enough to constitute an extremely serious problem in many companies today. I realize that I'm being quite harsh with some staff specialists who may be readers of this book, so let me temper my remarks to a degree and say that I don't blame these staff specialists too much for these actions. What I really blame is top management, which is frequently oblivious to the conditions that undermine supervisors' authority and effectiveness and does nothing about them.

COMMUNICATIONS

The dictionary defines communication as "an exchange of ideas through speech or writing." The key word in this sentence is "exchange." From the standpoint of this definition as it applies to the industrial community, management has done a miserable job of communicating with the people who can help it the most.

In more than 30 years that I have spent in the management consulting field, I have yet to find a company where the supervisory force felt that management was doing a good job of communications. When we approach supervisors on the subject of communications, we get only one answer: "Yes, they tell us what they want us to know. But that's where it stops. They never listen to us."

Management has concentrated on the downward side of communications and just about ignored the upward side of the picture. This hasn't worked. Management's present attitude of talking down to supervision is one of the major factors in the demoralization of the American supervisor.

It is vitally important that supervisors, as members of management, be kept continuously informed concerning changes in policy, organization, or conditions that affect their departments. They must receive the backing and support of higher management with reasonable speed. Yet in company after company we find that proposed changes manage to leak down to the rank and file before the first-line supervisor is even aware of them. In seven out of ten companies, union stewards know more about company policy than the supervisors do. There's been too much talk about communication and too little action.

I recall an incident that occurred during a presentation I gave to one of our largest metalworking trade associations. I made the statement that in four out of five companies today the union steward knows more about the contract than the supervisor. One of the presidents in the group took me up on this statement and said, "My supervisor has to watch production, keep costs down, watch quality, and on and on; how can he possibly know as much about the contract as the steward?" My answer to him was simply this: "Unfortunately, you are 100 percent right; however, take that attitude and you take the consequences. It's up to you to see that he knows."

Few companies take advantage of a supervisory newsletter, which can be mailed to a supervisor's home on a confidential basis. This gives the supervisor a feeling of being privy to things that are not available to the people he or she supervises. Too many companies feel that this is too costly or too much work. My feeling is that they cannot afford *not* to, from a standpoint of either time or money.

Only about 10 percent of today's organizations have taken the trouble to schedule monthly dinner meetings with first-line supervision, and in a good portion of these, the communication is mostly downward, with little credence being given to input from the supervisors themselves. To be effective, a meeting of this type must consist of a mutual exchange of ideas. It should also be attended by the sales manager, staff personnel, and the marketing manager.

If management is sincere about upgrading the role of the supervisor, it will be necessary to spend time to assure the supervisors that they are truly part of the organizational team. This, incidentally, must be top management's *own time*. It is a commodity that cannot be delegated to someone at a relatively low rung on the administrative totem pole.

A few years ago I conducted a survey of supervisors at a large midwestern utility plant. Fifty first-line supervisors were asked the question, "Why are some supervisors reluctant to exercise authority over employees under their jurisdiction?"

This was not a multiple-choice question. The participants had to think about and compose their replies. In spite of this, 36 out of the 50 supervisors who were queried stated that they did not feel that they had adequate backing from top management. Warranted or not, this attitude on the part of a majority of first-line supervisors is a clear indication that something is wrong. Regardless of the reasoning behind this thinking, top management should set the record straight, either by taking a greater interest in the supervisors' problems or by explaining to them the reasons for their apparent apathy.

SUPERVISOR SELECTION

In many instances the first-line supervisor in charge of a department is selected on the basis of qualifications that are entirely unrelated to criteria that define an effective supervisor. In four out of five companies where I served as a consultant, the supervisor had been promoted to the present job because he or she was the best machine operator or the senior person in the department. This practice may ruffle fewer feathers, but from a standpoint of maximum effectiveness any correlation between a good producer and a capable leader is purely coincidental.

If promotional policy of this type is followed (and there are, admittedly, some practical reasons for doing this), it is simply not enough to approach a worker on a Friday evening with the statement, "Joe, starting Monday morning you're taking over the department." Occasionally management might condescend to add, "There'll also be a $10.00 a week raise in it for you." However, the person selected may not even want the added responsibility. Assuming that he or she does, any promotion of this nature that is not followed up by a vigorous training program can be an open invitation to disaster.

The importance of this cannot be emphasized too strongly. In the course of numerous supervisor improvement programs in which I have participated over the years, we developed a series of questions designed to assess a supervisor's strong points and shortcomings. We later expanded the program to include shop stewards, which turned up an extremely interesting development: When the same questions were given to supervisors and union stewards in the 35 companies tested, the union stewards attained higher scores in such areas as mathematics, vocabulary, and practical judgment than did the supervisors. (see Fig. 4.1).

When we first analyzed these findings, the results seemed almost incomprehensible. However, a review of the situation made it

Figure 4.1. Compared Test Scores of Union Stewards and Company Supervisors

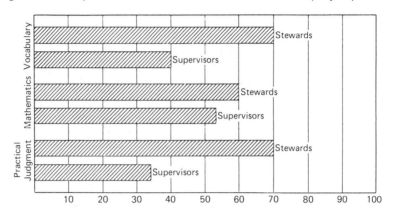

more understandable. After all, the stewards were usually selected by the democratic process for their ability to lead. On the other hand, most of the supervisors were in their present position because of seniority or because they were the most productive machine operator or best assembler.

In light of these findings, is it any wonder that the shop steward has in many instances managed to wrest the reins of leadership from the person who is being paid to run the show? Put another way: *If the supervisor doesn't lead, the shop steward will.*

Proper supervisor selection is a vital part of management's duties and responsibilities. During the selection process, management should consider a number of factors in addition to an employee's seniority and work record. To cite a few:

1. Make sure candidates have the leadership abilities required to make them good supervisors.
2. Be sure they want to be supervisors. Of today's supervisors, 25 percent never wanted to be supervisors in the first place.
3. Ensure them take-home play at least 20 percent greater than that of the skilled people who work for them.
4. Be sure they are people-conscious and will not lose sight of the fact that they are a part of management and responsible for company objectives.
5. Be certain they have enough self-confidence to be interested in doing a job instead of winning a popularity contest with employees.

6. Be sure they have training that is appropriate for the specific job and that helps correct their own particular weaknesses.

All these factors are vital to the making of a good supervisor. To the employee, the supervisor *is management.* And as a viable member of management he or she must have the necessary equipment to ensure a role of leadership.

If we are ready to admit that what America needs more than a good five-cent cigar is a good professional supervisor, I can heartily recommend a program that has been developed over the years, one that has been enormously successful in upgrading the effectiveness of supervision. The program has been used in literally dozens of widely diversified industries, and in no instance has it failed to result in a marked improvement in supervisory morale and effectiveness. For lack of a better term, I refer to this program as a supervisory inventory. It consists of determining the qualifications, needs, and attitudes not only of the supervisors, but of top management as well.

PART TWO: SOLUTION TO THE PROBLEM

Very few industrial leaders will deny that the first-line supervisor is industry's major problem. We will present in this section a program that has been extremely successful in upgrading the effectiveness of supervision in numerous companies.

It has been disturbing to witness the millions of dollars that industry spends every year on inventorying their materials and equipment and only a pittance on inventorying the most important asset—their key people. It has also been of concern to see how the average company readily associates employee morale with the production employee only and frequently uses morale surveys as a tool to measure this important aspect. Why not consider a supervisory assessment or supervisory inventory? This is where the action is and where it all starts—at the supervisory level.

Millions of dollars are spent every year by American management on supervisory training with the realization of very little in the way of results. In serving our clients, my firm, Patton Consultants, was concerned that our own training programs were not as fully effective as we believed they needed to be. We had fallen victim to a very common error. We had launched directly into a training program without first having evaluated the people to be trained. To correct this, we embarked on a program that initially analyzed their attitudes, listened to their concerns, and probed for their needs. We gained their enthusiastic support for the training program because the trainees participated in the planning of its scope and direction.

We found that through the application of these procedures management can be assured that it will attain the objectives it set out to achieve. Furthermore, we have found that, if management can convince the supervisors that it has their interests at heart and mean it, this will bring about more effective supervision than any incentive that could be devised.

Experience has demonstrated that this program goes a long way to dispel the "left out" feeling so commonplace among first-line supervision. It helps give them the feeling that management is interested in assisting them to do a better job and is willing to give them the necessary backing to accomplish this. Most importantly, they are made to feel that they are closer to and are in fact a part of management. Some procedures that foster these attitudes include having each person individually air his or her gripes; doing something about them; communicating more with each other; getting a better understanding of each other's problems; and, finally, having an opportunity to meet with top executives of other departments such as engineering and sales.

It is essential that there be emphasis on the primary importance of good supervision to the success of any manufacturing operation. The beneficial results that can be realized from various management programs—work measurement, standards and incentives, methods improvement and cost reduction, job classification and evaluation, and, particularly, a good program of labor relations—all assume the existence of a strong force of supervision and middle management.

OBJECTIVES

To design a tailor-made training program, an initial study or survey is necessary. This phase of the development program is called the Supervisory Inventory Analysis. This survey provides:

1. An assessment of the existing supervisory personnel.
   a. Their qualifications.
   b. Their performance and effectiveness, individually and collectively.
   c. Their problems.
   d. Their attitude and morale.
2. An assessment of the overall management climate, which either stimulates and encourages good performance or stifles it through misdirection or lack of interest.
3. A program to develop a more effective supervisory force by:
   a. Establishing criteria for the selection of future supervisors.
   b. Developing a meaningful training and development program for supervisors.
   c. Providing position descriptions that clearly spell out functions and responsibilities.
   d. Providing a program of supervisory compensation that includes a sound base salary supplemented by a motivating incentive.
   e. Providing goals and objectives with measurements of performance.

This preliminary phase is required to determine the existing conditions and problems as a basis for developing a training program.

DEVELOPMENT OF THE PROGRAM

Preliminary Evaluation of Personnel

First, prepare a list of people who will participate. In most cases it is recommended that the program include representatives from staff and service groups in the manufacturing areas, such as industrial engineering, design engineering, production planning and scheduling, and technical. Their participation can be useful for two reasons:

1. Staff and service functions are part of the climate in which the supervisor must work. Line and staff relationships frequently present serious problems.

2. Staff and service personnel are likely candidates for future line supervisors.

It is also recommended that a checklist of questions be prepared for top management to make sure that the information that is wanted is included. It is important to interview top management people to get an idea of the importance that management attaches to front-line supervision, what management expects from supervision, and what management expects from the Supervisory Inventory Analysis program.

Fig. 4.2 shows a questionnaire that has been used for this purpose.

Figure 4.2

QUESTIONNAIRE CHECKLIST FOR TOP MANAGEMENT

General Information

1. Selection of supervisors

    A.   Are all, or most, selections made from the ranks of the hourly workers?

    B.   Is the "good worker" with the "good attitude" who gets along well with people the prime candidate for supervisor?

    C.   Is technical know-how and experience in the shop the most important qualification?

    D.   Is the candidate fully apprised of the supervisor's job—the good and the bad?

    E.   Does the selection process determine if the candidate really desires to become a supervisor?

2. Training

    A.   Are supervisors given any training before assuming their duties?

    B.   Do they receive training after they assume their duties?

    C.   Do they fully understand their duties and responsibilities and where they fit in the management of the company?

3. Compensation
   A.   Are supervisors paid more than the people they supervise?
   B.   Will they be paid more after the workers go on incentive?
   C.   Is there a management policy regulating supervisory compensation?
4. General
   A.   Is there a written position description for the supervisor's job?
   B.   Does the supervisor have a unique set of duties and responsibilities, or does it appear at times that all levels of management are trying to do the supervisor's job?
   C.   Has management delegated to the supervisor the necessary authority to carry out his or her responsibilities?
   D.   Is the supervisor held accountable for his or her responsibilities?

Specific Questions Directed to the Individual Executive

1. What is your assessment of your first-line supervisory organization, superintendents and supervisors, as a group?
   A.   Are they effective? If not, why not?
   B.   Do you have confidence in them?
   C.   Are they doing the job you want done?
2. What do you think a supervisor's primary duties and responsibilities are? Number the following in order of importance:

Final detailed scheduling	Maintenance
Work assignments	Housekeeping
Performance and productivity	Eliminating and preventing delay
Control of quality	Safety
Control of costs	Employee/human relations
Control of expenses	Operator selection
Policing methods	Operator training
Systems and procedures	Grievance handling
Continuous improvement	

3. What role do you want the supervisor to play in the management of the company?
   A.   Do you see the supervisor as a manager of his or her area?
      1.   Concerned with costs and performance?
      2.   Involved in change and improvement? Or

    B.   Do you see the supervisor as an overseer who
        1.   Acts as a "pusher" or "straw boss" carrying out orders and decisions passed down to him or her?
        2.   Sees that things get done?

4. What role or function do you feel you should fill in regard to first-line management functions?
    A.   Do you monitor the roles of your immediate subordinates versus the supervisor?
    B.   Do you monitor the roles of various staff and service people versus the supervisor?

5. Do you think that incumbents are qualified by training and experience to do the job that should be done?

6. In your opinion:
    A.   Is the present policy or the methods for selecting supervisors compatible with the kind of supervisors needed?
    B.   Do you think any assurance against reverting to hourly ranks is appropriate when supervisors are selected from hourly classifications?

7. What kind of a background should a supervisor candidate have?
    A.   Should emphasis be on technical knowledge and ability to perform all the work supervised.?
    B.   Should emphasis be on ability to plan, train, set goals, measure, analyze, motivate, and improve?

8. What would you like to achieve from a supervisor's training program? (improved productivity, quality, morale)

9. What kind of specific training would you like the supervisors to receive?

Middle Management

As a part of the interview with the plant manager or superintendent in a larger organization, it is important that it be made clear that what is desired is the manager's own independent appraisal of all supervision with comparative rankings assigned. This may be used later for comparison with appraisals resulting from interviews.

    To assist in this, it is suggested the manager follow the method shown in the performance review in Fig. 4.3.

Figure 4.3

PERFORMANCE REVIEW

Name_____ Date_____
Jobtitle_____ Dept._____
Instructions[SL1Read carefully each of the factor descriptions and the explanations of each of the ratings. Rate each factor by circling the appropriate number. Rate only against the requirement of the *job listed above.*

Explanation of Ratings

5 Superior.
Constantly demonstrates a very desirable degree of the factor.

4 Above Average.
Well above minimum standards. Occasionally leaves something to be desired, but not often enough to be a problem.

3 Average.
Satisfactory. Would like more strength in this area. Not a serious problem now.

2 Below Average.
Marginally satisfactory at best. Needs improvement in this area or must compensate by strength in other areas.

1 Low.
A serious handicap to job performance.

BASIC FACTORS

A. *Job knowledge:* How complete are the individual's knowledge, skills, and abilities that are necessary in the performance of the job?

         5   4   3   2   1

B. *Motivaton:* What leve of energy, drive, and initiative is generally displayed in the pursuit of job goals?

         5   4   3   2   1

C. *Company relatedness:* To what extent does the employee relate himself with company policies, objectives, and problems?

         5   4   3   2   1

D. *Operating judgment:* How good is the individual's judgment in the practical problems that arise in connection with regular responsibilities?

5   4   3   2   1

E. *Leadership:* How effectively does the supervisor motivate subordinates to maximum effort? Does he or she stimulate subordinates to efficient work habits? Does he or she promote harmonious relationships among those under his or her supervision?

5   4   3   2   1

Summary and Conclusions:

What are the supervisor's positive qualities?
What are the supervisor's serious limitations?

Total points

On the basis of your appraisal, what is the individual's value to the company?

Point Range

23 to 25	Superior
18 to 22	Above average
13 to 17	Average
8 to 12	Below average
7	Low

The Interview

Plan and schedule an interview (one on one) with all supervisors, general supervisors, and superintendents. Prepare an appropriate questionnaire similar to the sample interview in Fig. 4.4 to use as a guide in these interviews.

Schedule all nonproduction supervisors, managers, and staff people who have been designated to participate in the program for a separate interview. Prepare an appropriate checklist similar to the Fig. 4.5.

Figure 4.4

INTERVIEW FOR PRODUCTION SUPERVISORS

1. How long with the company?
2. What jobs have you held with the company?
3. What else have you done?
    a. What other positions did you hold?
    b. How do you compare this company with other companies you have worked for?
4. How long have you been a supervisor?
5. Why do you think that you were picked to be a supervisor?
6. When you were offered a job as supervisor, did management tell you both the good and bad aspects of the job?
7. Do you think that you have received adequate training?
8. Do you receive adequate support from your superiors?
9. Do any of the workers you supervise earn as much or more than you do?
10. How good are your communications with:

    Employees   What is your primary source of
    Other supervisors   information?
    Your boss
    Management in general

11. Are you kept adequately informed on matters that are important to you?
12. Do you feel a part of the company management team?
13. Do you identify yourself more closely with the hourly people or with the management?
14. Do you undersand the:
        Labor contract
        Incentive manual
        Job evaluation program
        Company policies
        Company rules and regulations
    well enough to answer most questions that might come up?
15. Do you like being a supervisor?
16. Do you think that you are doing a good job?

17. What will it take to have you do a better job?
18. What do you dislike about your job?
19. What do you dislike about the company?
20. What do you like about the company?
21. What one thing would you like to see happen here?
22. What would you like to receive in the way of training?
23. What other improvements would you recommend for this company?
24. Do you think the size of the company is:

    a. Too large?
    b. Too small?
    c. About right?

25. Do you feel the company offers any opportunities for advancement?

Figure 4.5.

INTERVIEW FOR NONPRODUCTION EXECUTIVES

1. Your position?
2. How long have you been with company?
3. What else have you done?
4. How do you compare this company with others?
5. What do you like about this company?
6. What do you dislike about this company?
7. Do you believe the company is generally well managed?
8. Are you satisfied with the way your department is running?
9. What are the major problems?

Report of Findings and Recommendations

All the benefits expected from the supervisory analysis program are to be contained in the *Report of Findings and Recommendations*.

A. Findings

   1. Assessment of existing organization and personnel.

    a. Findings in regard to supervisory morale, and the attitudes of first-line supervision toward the company and toward their jobs, plus any particular problems.

    b. Findings with regard to how supervisors view themselves and their effectiveness.

    c. Rankings made by plant managers compared to results of study.

    d. Statement regarding the overall level of supervisory effectiveness—the good and the bad—and why.

2. Assessment of the management climate.

    a. Findings regarding how top management views first-line supervision.

    b. Findings dealing with how first-line supervision is actually used.

    c. The overall result of top management attitudes, policies, and practices as these things create a climate in which first-line supervision must exist.

B. Recommendations

1. A program to develop a more effective supervisory organization for the future, to include:

    a. Selection of future candidates.

    b. Training and development for both new and present supervisors.

    c. Duties and responsibilities.

    d. Goals and objectives.

    e. Measures of performance.

    f. Compensation.

2. Recommended changes in top management attitudes, policies and practices to encourage better supervisory performance.

NECESSARY ACTION BY MANAGEMENT

The next step is for management to back up the findings by *action*. Top management cannot afford to compacently sit back at this point and assume that it has done its part. Management must now engage in a vigorous program of setting an example for its supervisors. It must begin by recognizing that a portion of the blame for the supervisors' shortcomings must be laid at management's doorstep.

The questions contained in the top management survey, for example, will call for a large degree of soul-searching on the part of top managers. Most executives who approach this questionnaire with a positive attitude will find conditions that appear to call for some form of remedial action on their part. Human nature being what it is, some managers may even try to rationalize obvious shortcomings. But, make no mistake, whether they admit to these deficiencies or not, others in the organization will know about them and wonder why nothing is being done to correct them. No doubt establishment of better rapport between supervision and higher management will call for considerable time and effort. Yet managerial inaction is a trait that executives cannot afford to possess if they expect to continue in their present positions for very long.

Strong emphasis should be placed on developing a supervisory training program geared to alleviating areas where improvement is indicated as a result of the survey. Most supervisory training falls short of the mark for a variety of reasons. One of the biggest problems involves the fact that most supervisory training is conducted in a classroom and consists primarily of textbook guidelines that were designed to fit a multitude of problems that have little bearing on actual shop conditions. They consist, for the most part, of canned rhetoric delivered on a "talk-down" basis with little provision being made for student feedback. Additionally, these sessions are often conducted in a setting that tends to inhibit participants from contributing valuable input. To have maximum effect, a training program must be designed to fit actual shop conditions and problems as they exist on the supervisor's day-to-day job. This takes time and expense, but the rewards of tailoring a program to the needs of a specific organization can be tremendous.

Another shortcoming in many training programs is that all too frequently staff personnel, with whom the supervisor must work, have not been included. It is essential that these people be part of the program, if for no other reason than to make them aware of the unique problems faced by people on the firing line.

A major factor in the ultimate success of a training program can be enlisting the aid of some of the supervisors themselves in designating the subject matter to be discussed. It is also best to make it clear before the program begins that the curriculum will consist of workshop sessions rather than stereotyped lectures.

Supervisory meetings should be limited to not more than ten or fifteen supervisors; they should be conducted on company time during which the subjects in need of attention should be discussed in the order of importance.

One of the methods that can be used to determine subjects in need of attention is circulation of a Meeting Planning Questionnaire (Fig. 4.6) to all participants in the program. Based on the degree of interest shown in various categories, the person developing the program can then prepare a more meaningful agenda.

The questionnaire would vary from company to company and industry to industry. However, the following Meeting Planning Questionnaire and printout of training needs (Fig. 4.7) are typical and can be used as guidelines for the development of a training program.

The person conducting the supervisory training program should be an individual skilled in communications, especially in use of visual aids and other training devices. Any new solutions arrived at after a thorough discussion of the items in need of resolution should be written up, placed in a binder issued to each supervisor, and thereafter recognized as the official revised Policy Manual.

As I have stated many times, millions of dollars that have been spent on training with little assurance of results. In the early days of my management consultant career, we became quite conscious of this and were anxious to have tangible evidence that the training program fulfilled all the requirements outlined by management. What management must do is to follow up to determine the degree of success of the program through a repetition of the initial questionaires and interviews.

At the conclusion of phase 1 of the training program, the strengths and weaknesses are pinpointed for the supervisory, middle, and top management groups. From this information the training program is structured and conducted. This is phase 2. At the conclusion of the program, after a reasonable length of time, another check should be made or comparison made to see how these weaknesses were corrected and the strengths fortified. This affords management commonsense, down-to-earth accountability.

With a positive attitude by all parties concerned, and with a comprehensive program of supervisory training and development

Figure 4.6.

MEETING PLANNING QUESTIONNAIRE

I believe the training sessions would mean more to me if they included the items I have checked below.

Date_____   Supervisor_____

	CHOICE		
	1st	2nd	3rd
1. The supervisor as a part of management			
2. The responsibilities of a supervisor			
3. The responsibilities of a working leader..................			
4. The working leader's place in the plant organization........			
5. A study of our management organization			
6. A review of our Job Evaluation Program.................'....			
7. A review of our union contract			
8. How to analyze the distribution of work			
9. How to apply work distribution techniques			
10. How to study work methods for improvement			
11. How to understand and apply better work methods			
12. How to measure work			
13. How to receive, analyze, and plan work..................			
14. How to assign work, check work, and make reports			
15. How to set and use work standards			
16. How to deal with the new worker			
17. How to find and develop training needs			
18. How to develop a supervisor's pattern for job instruction ...			
19. A study of how differences in workers affect the job			
20. How to understand workers. Attitudes. Motivation.			
21. How to apply problem solving methods to human relations ...			
22. How to develop my leadership ability			
23. A plan for self improvement			
24. How to apply techniques of good human relations			
25. How to conduct individual and group discussions			
26. How to take corrective action on the worker's problems			
27. How to solve operating problems			
28. How to develop an understudy for our jobs			
29. How to make sound decisions			
30. How to communicate with the boss, the workers			

List below any items you would like touched upon.

31. _____

32. _____

33. _____

Figure 4.7.

SUBJECT AREA	▨ 1st Choice ▨ 2nd Choice	SURVEY OF TRAINING NEEDS

Self Development — 85%
Supervisors Place in Management — 77%
Human Relations — 76%
Technical Methods and Measurement — 74%
Assignment of Work — 72%
Development of Subordinates — 69%
Labor Contract and Job Evaluation — 30%

% 0 10 20 30 40 50 60 70 80

Chart Showing Degree of Interest in Major Subject Areas and Percent of First and Second Choice

based on organizational needs and accompanied by appropriate follow-through by *both* supervisors and management, supervisory effectiveness *can* be attained. A word of caution, though. Top management may, by virtue of its rank, consider itself to be in a position immune from serious participation and may therefore assume an attitude of inaction or only superficial support. If this is done, the program will not be effective.

It takes "big" human beings to recognize and remedy deficiencies in their own performance when they may feel they are in a strong enough position to overlook them without jeopardizing their job. But the managers who make a sincere attempt to judge themselves by the same criteria that they apply to subordinates will be the ones who benefit most from a program of this type. I can personally attest to the fact that this program has resulted in a marked upgrading of first-line supervisors in literally dozens of companies.

At one of these companies, McCreary Tire and Rubber Company, Harry C. McCreary, chairman of the board, offered three observations on things that made the program a success in his organization.

1. Be certain to let every supervisor and staff member know that the top executive is behind the program.
2. Convince the group that their honest answers are needed.
3. Most important, it is essential that management correct any faults or weaknesses that are brought to light through the program. Also important, if management is not in a position to correct the weaknesses, it should be explained why they cannot.

THE ROAD AHEAD

The importance of the first-line supervisor to any meaningful improvement in the industrial status quo cannot be overemphasized. The current emphasis on "excellence in business" will, within the next few years, generate a long overdue increase in programs designed to recognize the first-line supervisor as a major force in the shape of things to come. When this happens, it should also include recognizing these individuals in the area of status, compensation, and promotional opportunity.

Should the movers and shakers of today's industry fail to do this, the status of the supervisor will continue to be summed up by a sign that hangs over the desk of a shift supervisor in a Detroit auto plant:

> They don't let me run the train,
>   the whistle I can't blow.
> I'm not allowed to work the switch,
>   or make the engine go.
> I'm not allowed to let off steam,
>   or even ring the bell.
> But let the damn thing jump the track,
>   and see who catches hell.

5

Assuring Results
through Accountability

Pity the overworked executive! Behind his
paperwork ramparts, he struggles bravely with a
seemingly superhuman load of responsibilities.
Burdened with impossible assignments, beset
by constant emergencies, he never has a
chance to get organized. Pity him—but
recognize him for the dangerous liability that he
is.

Clarence B. Randall

I had the opportunity to initiate an accountability program many years ago before numerous books were written under formal titles such as Management by Objectives, Long and Short Range Planning, Strategic Planning, and the like. For the lack of a better term, I have labeled this program Assuring Results through Accountability. The reason I like this title is that executive accountability is the grass-roots basis for accomplishing end results for any company, no matter what the title of the program might be.

I developed this program, or technique, while serving as a professional director and advisor to W. F. Rockwell, Jr., president of Rockwell Manufacturing Co., now part of Rockwell International.

The scope of my duties required assuming responsibility for ultimate results without formal authority. To do this, it was quite obvious that:

1. I would have to get results through other people.
2. I would not be in a position to give orders.
3. I would have to lay out the road map for positive direction.
4. I would have to assure the end results.

The program was so successful that it has since been used, with appropriate modifications, at numerous large and small organizations with results that more often than not exceeded original expectations.

Why was it successful? On the basis of my observations of the inner workings of literally hundreds of different companies in virtually all areas of modern industry, I would say that one single factor separates the outstanding organizations from the mediocre ones. Top management in the outstanding companies requires—and demands—accountability of everyone, from the janitor to the company president. On the basis of 30 years experience as a consultant, I can state unequivocally that I have never experienced a tool of management that comes as close to guaranteeing results as a properly devised executive accountability program.

To set the stage properly for an explanation of this technique, it might be well at this point to consider a few typical examples involving lack of accountability.

• Your bank statement shows a debit balance that you know to be in error. A hassle follows. Finally the bank manager acknowledges the mistake. "It's a computer error," he tells you. "Sorry."

• Necessary parts for assembling a manufactured product have been faithfully promised in ten days. Two weeks later they have not arrived. The assembly line grinds to a halt. You call the contractor. "We've been snowed under," he tells you blandly. "Give us another week and we'll have them at your plant."

• A plane crashes short of the runway at a major airport. Minutes earlier another aircraft reported what appeared to be a tornado along the landing flight path. No one in the tower bothers to relay the information to other planes in the vicinity. One hundred and thirty-five people are killed. The tragedy is blamed on wind shear.

Does Anyone Really Care about Accountability Anymore? Each of the preceding incidents is completely different in nature, yet remarkably similar in a single respect. They involve people who are reluctant to accept accountability for actions that adversely affect normal operations.

While few statistics are available on the subject, lack of accountability must rank among the major problem areas in our industrial scene. It inhibits productivity, causes customer dissatisfaction, increases costs, and often generates expensive and time-consuming lawsuits. Curiously, the problem appears to be particularly prevalent at the supervisory and executive levels where management people, burdened with fewer monitoring procedures, often find it easy to alibi away the results of poor decisions.

Executive accountability is the most underrated and overlooked management tool in American industry. If this sentence sounds like an overstatement, consider the fact that many organizations spend hundreds of thousands of dollars measuring the worker on the bench or a $250-a-week machine operator, but they never give a second thought to the need for some yardstick to measure the performance of a $60,000-a-year sales manager or plant superintendent.

In my observation of hundreds of companies representing widely diversified industries, I have been continually amazed at the number of executives who are paid high salaries for expertise in executive analysis who fail to recognize that management cannot always be permitted to march to the beat of its own drummer. In some instances this policy of regarding managers as a superelite group who are exempt from the same set of standards that they apply to subordinates can be charged to simple ego. More often than not, however, it is caused by a failure to recognize how much an organization has expanded. Subtly and imperceptibly, operations often get too big and complex to be guided by the random advice and counsel of whatever select hierarchy happens to be situated near the top of the administrative totem pole at the moment. When this happens, it is time for management to realize that it can no longer afford the luxury of operating under an industrial caste system. At that time accountability standards must be developed, not only at the lower rungs of the administrative echelon but for all members in the organization.

Failure to recognize the need for executive accountability can sometimes be attributed to management advisors who, to put it bluntly, are brought in to find out what went wrong by the people who made it go wrong. Even when these management advisors recognize the problem, they are often reluctant to criticize the people who pay their fees. This is certainly not standard practice among all management advisors, but it happens often enough to constitute a real problem in many organizations.

The time is long since past when any organization can meet the competition with a random set of rules based on the dubious premise that management can be depended on to do the right thing simply because it had been vested with the authority to make decisions. At some point in an organization's development, whether it be through mergers, growth, diversification, or increased competition, a company can no longer put up with a game plan that entails outguessing the competition. Instead, the competition must be *outplanned*. Management must also be held accountable for both making and executing plans. Put another way, planning, unless accompanied by accountability, is as worthless as the message in a Chinese fortune cookie.

LONG- AND SHORT-RANGE PLANNING

Two extremely fashionable subjects these days are long- and short-range planning. Enough literature has been written on both of these subjects to fill a good portion of the Grand Canyon. And, sad to state, as far as attaining the intended results is concerned, much of this material might as well have been dispatched directly to that location.

Planning is necessary to the financial stability of an organization. Most financial institutions today require and demand that a company have a long-range planning program before they will grant a loan. All too often, however, planning projects go down to defeat after the first few skirmishes because they are poorly conceived, are inadequately implemented, and fail to include the proper degree of individual responsibility. It is also vitally important that the program be thoroughly sold to those poeople responsible for its success.

Each company is a unique entity, not only because of the people who make up its personnel, but also because of its environment, the organization itself, its products, the industry in which it operates, and the resultant conditions of change. Therefore, for any planning project to acquire an acceptable degree of success requires an awareness of all these conditions, coupled with a thorough understanding of the general criteria of effective implementation.

Development of a viable planning program is not something that can be done as an interesting interlude between sales meetings. It is a difficult and complex endeavor that can be successful only if it is pursued vigorously over an extended period of time. Most short-range planning projects will have a duration of one year, or possibly longer. In the case of long range planning, the program usually extends for five years. It is the uncertain developments that occur during this lengthy time span that cause many planning projects to gradually deteriorate and eventually disintegrate under their own weight when well-intentioned goals and objectives are sabotaged by unforeseen problems and unexpected developments.

For the company that wants to begin planning but hasn't done it up to now, evolution is too slow and revolution is too fast. Therefore, one significant question arises: Is there any sure-fire method by which an organization can embark on a planning project and be assured of favorable results?

The answer to this seemingly loaded question is an emphatic yes! It is by the installation of an accountability program.

When Rockwell, who was always a strong advocate of employee accountability, introduced the accountability plan at his manufacturing plant, company officials suggested he may have gone too far. His reply was, "Good men *want* to be held accountable. Mediocre men *must* be held accountable."

Time proved that Rockwell's philosophy was valid. Following the implementation of the program, the company went on to achieve the lowest cost in the industry, with the highest earnings for its employees. The balance of this chapter will explain exactly how this program works.

THE ASSURED RESULTS PLANNING
PROGRAM

Reduced to its simplest form, Assuring Results through Accountability consists of a step-by-step method for accomplishing assured
results, with each step of the process laced with large portions of
accountability. Admittedly, establishing and meeting executive
standards of accountability are not always easy tasks to achieve.
Spontaneous acceptance of the need for increased performance by
key people is often a pill that is difficult to digest. But if the steps
outlined in this chapter are diligently followed, a successful program can be developed with extremely favorable results. Furthermore, the people who might initially regard the program
unenthusiastically often turn out to be its biggest backers.

Most planning programs fall apart for a variety of reasons, in
addition to failure to include a proper degree of accountability. In
designing a program, many managers fail to take the time to find
out exactly where they are at present and where they intend to go.
In some instances program goals are assigned to subordinate managers on the basis of personality traits, rather than on the basis that
management behavior is more important than personality. Additionally, goals and objectives are frequently based on meaningless
criteria and fuzzy concepts that do little to describe the actual improvement required or the time frame in which this must be accomplished. Still other pitfalls include failure to lay proper groundwork,
to secure motivation, to adequately describe organizational responsibilities, and to delegate the proper degree of authority.

Assuring Results through Accountability is specifically designed to eliminate all these common problems. It consists of five
separate steps:

1. Developing a management inventory
2. Developing corporate objectives
3. Establishing goals
4. Converting goals to specific projects
5. Assuring the program's success

For purposes of clarification, the term *objectives* as used in this
text refers to corporate objectives as set forth by top management
and/or the board of directors. *Goals* refer to the agreed-upon targets

to be accomplished by individual managers within the organization. *Projects* refer to the ways and means of accomplishing these goals.

These steps can be implemented most effectively if they are performed separately in the order shown. In some instances, however, where no lines of authority overlap, it may be logical and expedient to proceed to the next step in a department or division before all the details of the previous step have been finalized by the entire organization.

Either way, the first step in the program should be developing a management inventory.

Developing a Management Inventory

Whether it is conducted as a massive project in a large corporation like General Motors or as a superficial check by a small shopkeeper, the process of conducting a periodic inventory is an indispensable part of the American business machinery. It is doubtful whether any firm could long survive without this inventory.

Yet while virtually all companies have some form of inventory mechanism, most of them fail to include one component that is vital to the future success of the organization. Specifically, they fail to include a comprehensive listing of exactly where improvement can be most effectively achieved, plus an assessment of what can be expected of individual managers in accomplishing these improvements.

Preparation of a management inventory will do more than simple advise top management of areas where marked improvement can be expected. It will also help convince individual managers that the chief executive officer is serious about the proposed planning project. Additionally, it will generate enthusiasm for the program from managers who in participating in the management inventory will be forced to think about ways the program can be more effectively implemented.

Over the years, numerous planning programs have appeared on the industrial horizon. They go by names like "management by objectives," "management by results," "long- and short-range planning," "standards of accountability," and other titles. Many of these programs are based on generally sound principles and can often be expected to achieve a degree of success. However, in all the books and magazine articles that have been written on this subject, if there is one plan that contains more than a superficial mechanism for

determining exactly where improvement can be expected, it has es-
caped my notice and been conspicuous by its absence.

In its simplest form, planning consists of determining where
we want to go. However, it's extremely difficult to find out where
we want to go unless we first know where we are. Hence the need
for a management inventory.

A management inventory should consist of a series of
questionaires covering four basic subjects: plant capacity planning,
market planning, product planning, and financial planning. Understandably, the actual distribution of these questionnaires, plus the
type of questions they contain, will vary somewhat depending on
the organization and the types of products or services it offers. Nevertheless, the basic theme should be to permit managers to analyze
their present operation coldly and unemotionally, in terms of improvement. In developing the questions, no attempt should be
made to obtain simple yes-or-no answers. Rather, the wording
should force the managers to think out their replies and give personal views and opinions.

Prior to distributing the questionnnaires it should be pointed
out to each individual manager that there are no right or wrong answers. They should be assured that the study is designed to stimulate ideas for improvement that can be later converted to goals and
then into projects, which, when executed correctly, will help them
to reach departmental goals. Additionally, they should be in-
structed to analyze each situation unemotionally and without regard to personalities except as they directly influence the solution to
the problem. They should be informed that the questions have been
constructed to stimulate thinking on a wide variety of subjects and
the relationships of these subjects to their department. Also, in the
event that they feel there are circumstances beyond their control,
they should be encouraged to answer frankly.

Lists of suggested questions designed for each of the four basic
categories noted follow:

Plant Capacity Planning

1.Please describe the present plan of organization in your department and show the revisions you think are necessary to strengthen
or correct weaknesses. Do you believe that all key jobs are adequately staffed and that there is proper strength in the second and

third echelons of management? Are there functions essential to present operations that are not yet a part of your organization?

2. Is your industrial engineering department adequately staffed and functioning properly? If not, why not?

3. Explain the strengths and weaknesses of your present work operation area. Do you have a surplus or shortage of floor space? Is there a need to replace major equipment? If so, explain why and estimate its cost. Has the use of other facilities been properly considered? Explain.

4. How recently has your present work area layout been checked? What has been done? What needs to be done? What layout changes would have to be made to *decrease* costs and *increase* production? Explain.

5. Has a program of simplification of paper work and elimination of forms been instituted? When? Is it effective? How do you know?

6. Has a program to check the effectiveness of tooling been installed? Has it been checked recently? When?

7. Is there an effective program of preventive maintenance? Document results since it has been in operation.

8. If applicable, describe your program for quality control. Is there a scrap control program? What percentage of scrap do you have now as compared to the past three years?

9. Is the inventory control function maintaining stocks of finished goods, raw materials, and supplies at levels adequate to meet production and sales requirements and at the same time to avoid unnecessary use of working capital? Describe the method used to ensure balanced inventories. What turnover does your department get by major product line per year? What do you consider good performance? Why? If present performance is not meeting standard, how do you explain it?

10. Is obsolescence of parts checked periodically? What have been the results of this check for the past year?

11. Does our sales department provide our production department with adequate forecasts for production control and scheduling? If not, why not? Describe current programs to improve these forecasts and how they are coordinated with the sales division.

12. Does our plant have the machine-hours and worker-hours to permit effective scheduling? If not, what should be done to allevi-

ate this problem? are parts and operations sheets complete? If not, how should they be modified?

13. Is the question of "make or buy" raised periodically? If not, why not? If so, what were the results? Do you feel that purchasing and production are properly coordinated? If not, what should be done to alleviate this problem?

14. Are production standards and/or wage incentives being properly utilized? What percentage of your direct workers are covered? Do you think the present standards or wage incentives Are effective for maximum productivity? If not, what should be done to correct them?

15. Is indirect labor covered by standards? If so, what percentage? If no, why not? Is machine downtime recorded and accounted for? How is this done?

16. Are cost figures available by product and by operation? Is the factory cost system functioning as an effective management tool?

17. What has been done to be certain that subordinate managerial and supervisory personnel are aware of company policies?

18. Explain the advantages and disadvantages of your department's program for selecting and upgrading personnel. Are you satisfied that this is working well? What can you suggest to improve it?

19. Are our plant wage and salary practices in line with our policies and with community rates? Give details if you believe there are problems.

20. Do you have a program for job evaluation? If not, why not? If so, what has been done to be certain it is being maintained? If wage incentives are used, how are they being maintained? Have written policies for their maintenance been established? If so, show examples. If not, why not? Is there a program of merit rating? If so, describe it. If not, why not?

21. Do you know what the present attitudes of your employees are? What methods have you used to determine employee attitudes? Have you taken corrective action on legitimate complaints? What have you done to ensure that communications are a two-way street? Does your department have an employee handbook? If not, when will you have one? Is an effective suggestion system in operation? Cite results.

22. What types of training programs are presently in use? What are the strengths and weaknesses of the existing programs?

23. What is your employee turnover and how does it compare with the area and the industry? What can you suggest to improve it?

24. Cite any additional ideas you may have about how our staff can be of more value in helping you attain short- and long-range program goals.

Market Planning

1. Who, or what group in your department, determines the product needs of your department and the markets you serve? Do you feel that this responsibility is correctly assigned at present and that the procedure is working with maximum effectiveness? If so, explain why. If not, explain why not and what you suggest for improvement. Do you feel that there is any corporate or outside influence that is preventing your department from doing an outstanding job in this area?

2. Are you confident that you know the current demand for your major product lines in the markets you serve? What sources do you use to get this information? Do you believe you and your organization are doing a good job of recognizing new applications for existing products in present or new markets? Why? Do you feel that you can predict total demand your share of market for major product lines for the next three years with reasonable accuracy? Why or why not?

3. Do you feel that products produced in your department have product superiority over competition? If so, tell why by product line. If not, why not?

4. What do you believe to be the current opinion of your customers about your major product lines? How do you know? Can you define your dollar and percentage share of each major market during the past three years? If so, please do so. If you think customers are critical of one or more of your lines, please describe and give your opinion about why. Can you suggest changes to correct this? What keeps you from making those changes now?

5. Who determines pricing policies for the product lines in your department? How often are prices reviewed? Describe your procedure for setting and adjusting unit and parts prices. If you sell service, how do you determine price? Are you satisfied that you base pricing decisions on adequate information? Explain. What improvements can you suggest for better pricing control and price-setting methods?

6. Describe your policies for functions such as the establishment of credit terms, trade discounts, and quantity discounts. Are these policies clearly defined in writing for your sales group and customers? If not, why not? What evidence do you have that these policies are followed?

7. Who develops sales policies in your division, and how are they communicated to the salesperson level? How do you know that these policies are communicated and understood? What is the method of obtaining sales leads? What are the extent and intensity of supervision of individual sales personnel? Do you think sales techniques and salesperson supervision could be improved? How? What keeps you from doing this?

8. Please list your principal competitors and document their strengths and weaknesses. What do you believe to be the market acceptance of competitive products? How have you determined this? Describe any abnormal competitive practices. Are you satisfied that your sales management and field groups really know what competitors are offering customers? What evidence do you have this is so? If you believe improvement is required in this area, what suggestions can you offer?

9. Do you personally participate in forming policy and planning for advertising, publicity, trade shows, and product promotion schemes? How do you rate these programs against similar programs offered by the competition? What could be done to improve them? Do you feel that budgetary or outside influences keep you from doing an outstanding job in these areas? Explain. Is there good coordination between promotion programs and direct selling? Give positive or negative examples.

10. Are you satisfied with the timing and technical quality of bulletins, spec sheets, instruction manuals, service manuals, and parts lists for new products in your department? Explain with examples. If not, suggest improvements.

11. Please state your views in detail concerning the best methods for selection of sales personnel. Are we presently using these methods? If not, why not? Do you believe your sales organization is well balanced from an age and experience level? Give details, please. Can you suggest any improvements you would make if you had a completely free hand?

12. Please state your views in detail on the best methods of training and retaining sales managers and sales personnel. Are you satisfied with our current programs? If not, why not? How do you

judge the effectiveness of training methods currently in use? Give examples of existing programs.

13. Describe current methods for forecasting sales by product line and setting individual sales quotas. Do you believe these methods to be effective? How could they be improved? Are you satisfied with your sales call and sales cost-reporting systems? If so, why? If not, why not?

Product Planning

1. Describe the engineering appraisal procedure in use in your department for key engineering personnel. Do you think this procedure is satisfactory? If so, why? If not, what can be done to improve it?

2. What means of communication have been set between engineering, manufacturing, sales, and other departments? Do you feel that current communications procedures are satisfactory? If so, how do you know? If not, why not?

3. What is your basic policy for development of new products and major product redesigns in your department? What major new products have been developed and what have they contributed to annual sales volume in each of the past five years? Please estimate what proportion of the product line volume for the last year came from sale of products not in the line ten years ago. Are you satisfied with this? Why or why not? What steps do you think should be taken to improve your research and product development program?

4. What basic design policies exist in your department and how have you made your organization aware of them? Does the design group give good consideration to manufacturing costs in design? What evidence do you have to support your answer? Does your design group have a good grasp of competitive designs? What's your feeling about this group's performance compared to your toughest competition?

5. Have you instituted programs among engineering, purchasing, and manufacturing, such as value analysis or substitution of better or less costly materials? If not, why not? If so, what evidence do you have that these programs are paying off?

6. Describe the procedures you have installed for product testing. Have standards been set for product quality relative to practical attainment and competitive products? Give examples. Are you

satisfied with existing testing procedures in terms of information obtained and costs involved? What can you suggest for improvement?

7. Can you describe outstanding exclusive features of recent product introductions that you feel indicate above-average engineering accomplishments? Do you feel that style is being given as large a share of attention as performance? On what do you base this reasoning? How does the competition fare in this area?

Financial Planning

1. Describe how you evaluate international, national, and industry trends and translate your thinking on these matters into departmental actions.

2. Do you foresee major changes in any of the following areas that would have a material effect on your financial planning?

Technology

Customer demands

Competition

Pricing

Taxes

Government regulations

If so, please explain.

3. What steps are being taken to improve the following?

Annual and long-range budgeting

Capital spending estimates

Cash-flow estimates for financial control and cost-system improvement

4. What progress is being made on mechanized machine accounting? Are you satisfied with current efforts? If not, how would you improve them?

5. Are distribution costs under constant review to your satisfaction? If so, what method is used?

6. Are plant expenditures periodically reviewed to determine whether they are justified in view of changing conditions?

7. Are manufacturing expenses controlled through specific budget accounts?

8. Have the insurance requirements of our plant been reviewed for adequacy of coverage, correctness of values, and reasonableness of costs? If not, why not?

9. Are credit and collection policies established and communicated to marketing? What inadequacies do you feel exist? How do you suggest they be corrected?

The preceding questions are not all-inclusive, but they give an idea of the basic *types* of questions that should be asked. These questions, you will note, are generally designed to stimulate *thinking* on the part of individual managers on topics that can later be translated into workable goals.

Top management and the people selected to guide the planning program should make a comprehensive review of the composite replies. It will be almost certain to pinpoint areas where improvement can be expected. Armed with a comprehensive list of areas for possible improvement plus a complete inventory of departmental strengths and weaknesses, the person in charge of the planning project will now be in a position to structure the program in a manner designed to ensure that agreed-upon goals are consistent with the abilities of the individual managers who will be charged with the responsibility for accomplishing these goals.

Even more importantly, conducting a management inventory as described will lay the groundwork to enable an organization to develop and implement a planning program based on accountability techniques and tailored to individual managerial thinking.

Developing Corporate Objectives

Before even attempting to establish any future goals for key personnel who participated in the management inventory, it is imperative that top management and/or the board of directors agree on a set of company objectives that can later be used as a basis for developing departmental goals.

The importance of establishing meaningful and workable objectives cannot be overemphasized. Most companies have already established some objectives. However, all too frequently they are based on wishful thinking or superficial data. In some cases, they may even consist of meaningless propaganda designed to pacify the company's stockholders.

To be effective, any company objective must be based on solid, workable data and should conform to the following guidelines:

1. *It must be practical.* Does it really represent a marked benefit for the total organization, or is it simply a sacred cow that has been insisted on by a single section or department?

2. *It must be suitable.* Are you heading in the right direction? You can't set an objective to sell more buggy whips when people no longer drive buggies.

3. *It must be acceptable.* The people who are needed to turn an objective into a reality must be sold on its practicability.

4. *It must be economically feasible.* Is it worth the price in money and worker-hours that could be used to better advantage elsewhere?

5. *It must be attainable.* You can't build a spaceship in a blacksmith shop no matter how strong the motivation. The management inventory can be an invaluable tool in determining attainability.

6. *It must be measurable.* Wherever possible an objective should be stated in quantitative terms. "Reduce unit manufacturing cost" is a fuzzy concept. "Reduce unit manufacturing cost from $10.50 per unit to $9.25" is unmistakable and suited to subsequent measurement.

Here is a sample list of corporate objectives that meets all the requirements just described.

1. To utilize the total assets and resources of the company to increase the earnings per share. The objective for the current year is $1.60 per share.

2. To realize a company return on investment of at least 15 percent of total assets before taxes while generating the maximum cash flow.

3. To grow by investment of capital assets and major expense in new products, by development or acquisition, that increase the corporate return on investment by a minimum of 5 percent.

4. To spend up to 3 percent of sales on the development of new and/or improved products to increase our penetration of current markets.

5. To utilize our manufacturing capacities at a minimum average of 50 percent.

6. To discontinue obsolete and/or unprofitable product lines that represent dying business.

7. To increase market penetration by 5 to 10 percent depending on product line.

8. To be recognized as the leader in the market for both quality products and services.

9. To recognize the significance of total abilities and total costs when evaluating opportunities for new product development or acquisitions.

10. To recognize the different characteristics of our different kinds of businesses and to find the most effective method of operating each of these businesses within the framework of overall corporate objectives.

11. To diversify by development or by acquisition into added multicustomer markets that meet the prior corporate objectives.

Establishing Goals

Once corporate objectives are firmly fixed, the next step is for subordinate managers to establish goals to meet these objectives. Before this can be accomplished it is absolutely essential to create the proper climate. If the proper climate does not exist, it is doubtful whether the program will ever really amount to much.

Climate encompasses many things. It includes the ability of subordinates to express basic disagreements without reprisals from superiors. It includes a real attempt on the part of supervisors to search for, rather than skim over, possible disagreements between themselves and those under their jurisdiction. It includes acceptance of the fact that managers' stature will not suffer if their thinking is modified by others.

Usually, a chief executive wants to set goals to achieve improvements. Unfortunately, approaching subordinates on that basis will often negate any possible benefits. Top management should refrain from advancing its own ideas or even suggesting possible goals.

The program cannot be regarded as a necessary evil by the people who must make it work. The key to success is the magic quality of desire. And instilling this ingredient takes an intensive orientation program in which subordinates can develop an appreciation of what specific goals can do for *them.* The program can be guided by someone else, but management *must* participate, and management *must* be sold on the program.

In this stage the advantages to subordinates, the potential of increased earnings, the spirit of competition, and the opportunity for advancement through company growth can be stressed. The learning process will be more effective if subordinates receive the same reading material that is circulated among top management.

The greatest emphasis should be on the fact that the departmental goals developed to achieve the stated corporate objectives will be set by the person whose performance is going to be evaluated during the course of the program. Once the goals are established, of course, they can usually be rephrased or restated by the chief executive. But if top management sets the standards first, it may abort the entire program.

When working with people who have never set goals before, it is better to give them an overall view of the program in the first session and then give them time to think about it. Several meetings a few weeks apart are preferable to one long session. Because each manager will be responsible for setting his or her own goals, a responsibility checklist must be developed. The list should state exactly which key personnel are to be made responsible for improvement in the various areas where more effective performance is indicated. This list need not be extremely complex, but it should be pertinent to the specific job. If the superior and subordinate prepare the list jointly, it usually turns out to be a developmental experience for both of them. It is important to avoid the pitfall of listing personal traits rather than examining specific issues and end results. No confusion or misunderstanding can be allowed regarding responsibility or authority in any area. Insofar as possible, the organization should strive to avoid overlapping of responsibility or authority by several departments or individuals.

A word of caution here. I recall an old Arabian Nights tale in which the protagonist, a poor peasant boy, was asked about his goals in life. He said he wanted to become the richest man in the kingdom, become ruler of the entire empire, and marry a princess. In the story he attains all three of these goals. This, of course, was only a fairy tale. I cite it to point out that one of the pitfalls in permitting managers to set their own goals is that, contrary to what you might expect, they often set them too high. Their optimism in some instances may be sparked by a genuine enthusiasm for goal setting. In other cases it may result from the simple desire to tell top management something they feel it would like to hear. In either case this can be a built-in booby trap, particularly if top management compounds the problem by accepting a set of next-to-impossible guidelines. Problems will develop later when the initial guidelines must be modified, because this may set a precedent for watering down the entire program.

The real catalyst that makes a program successful is strict accountability. Members of the organization should all be fully aware that they are in business for themselves. It is also important to hold regular meetings, preferably monthly, to ensure that the timetable for goal setting is being maintained. Since the goals were set by the individuals responsible for maintaining them, contingencies should have been taken into account. In other words, there is no acceptable excuse for nonperformance!

Once departmental goals are tentatively established, it is important at this point for top management to review the goals developed for each department or division to ensure that their sum total adds up to the corporate objectives established earlier.

Converting Goals to Specific Projects

When I functioned as a professional director, it disturbed me to note that the designers of most long- and short-range planning programs end their efforts when the design stage is over and hope that subordinates and key personnel will be sufficiently motivated and qualified to follow through with the necessary implementation. Unfortunately, it is not that easy. This is the precise point where a program of this type will begin to deteriorate unless additional steps are taken.

Successful implementation of the program requires that the goals established earlier now be converted into specific projects— which frequently may include subprojects. Each project plan will describe the end result to be accomplished in quantitative terms, including the time needed for completion. Bench marks will have to be established in advance. A six-month project, for example, will contain six bench marks so that the status of the project can be determined at successive monthly meetings.

Because the problems in various organizations are so diversified, it is unlikely that any two could be solved by the same form of remedial action. For the sake of illustration, let's assume that one department in a particular company set a goal of lowering production costs by 15 percent within the next 12 months. Suppose further that the basis for this goal is that the competition is spending much less on operational costs.

The obvious action must be to translate that goal into specific projects to be finalized as outlined earlier in this chapter. Specific projects for accomplishment of the goal could be any or all of the following:

Better incentive coverage

Measurement of indirect labor costs

Work simplification program

Standardization of parts

Improved tooling

Better materials handling

Even the most superficial analysis of these six projects will determine that most of them will also involve subprojects. For example, the work simplification program will probably entail a detailed analysis of the work operations performed by all key personnel, including the supervisors, the assistant supervisors, and the setup workers. It would be conducted by the staff engineering department from headquarters and would also include a value analysis program by the plant industrial engineering department. Staffing tables would have to be developed by staff industrial engineering, along with cost estimates, techniques of accomplishment, and a quantitative outline of what had to be accomplished in a fixed period of time.

Because of the complex nature of achieving many of these goals and projects, it is imperative that a logical step-by-step procedure be set up at this time to accomplish the prestated aims and assure successful implementation of the program. The following step-by-step procedure has been used successfully by many companies and is recommended for assuring that the program will achieve the desired results.

Assuring the Program's Success

Immediately following the establishment of departmental goals, a meeting should be held with all department heads. At this meeting these key managers should be informed that they will have many problems to solve in meeting their respective goals. For example, if the vice-president of operations has a goal of reducing labor costs by 15 percent in the next 12 months, he or she will have the problems of scrap control, reducing both direct and indirect labor, and reducing overtime costs.

The managers should then be informed of the steps to be taken to accomplish these goals and how to resolve the problems that may arise during implementation of the program. Each company goal or problem encountered as part of that goal must be interpolated into projects in the following manner:

1. Obtain a thorough, detailed description of the problem.
2. Determine and describe what is to be accomplished.
3. Determine if there are any subprojects needed to accomplish the primary project. If so, assign a person or people to determine subprojects.
4. Determine the technique of accomplishment. It is very important to think this through, for many reasons. If this is not done, it will be difficult to determine the worker-hours needed to accomplish the project and also to schedule the completion date.
5. Carefully determine the worker-hours needed to complete the project.
6. Establish a cost estimate to complete the project.
7. Estimate savings or nonmonetary results.
8. Place priorities on multiple projects.
9. Establish bench marks. If the project is to take six months, six specific bench marks must be determined in advance in order to determine the status of projects at succeeding monthly meetings.

During this same meeting the managers should be cautioned to be certain to analyze each project thoroughly and completely for possible subprojects and for possible problems that could change the time schedule or overall results. They should also be warned to allow adequate time and to look out for necessary information required from other people or departments. They must be certain that projects represent genuine improvements, not just a part of day-to-day operations, and that not too many projects are undertaken.

Managers must make sure that everyone involved understands all the implications of the project and that all concerned are prepared to meet unforeseen difficulties that may tend to stand in the way of completing the project in the indicated time frame. Finally, managers must see that all employees, including subordinates, have gone through the same thorough analysis process to ensure that they, in turn, will accomplish the desired end results.

A second meeting should be held in approximately three to four weeks, at which time each member will make a presentation of his or her project or projects, a definition of what is to be accomplished, an identification of any accompanying subprojects, a comprehensive overview of how the project will be accomplished, a presentation of the monthly bench marks, and a statement of the final completion date. During this second meeting, all members should be reminded that each member has been permitted to determine his or her own method by which to accomplish the end results. Each member has been permitted to determine his or her own time schedule, and each member has been permitted to determine what and how much is to be accomplished. Therefore, no excuses will be acceptable for not accomplishing end results since each person has been given adequate opportunity to allow for contingencies. For maximum effect, this speech should be made by the president or a delegate of the president.

During the rest of the program, meetings should be held on a schedule geared to the bench marks that were determined earlier. At these meetings, members should present the current status of their projects. Throughout the entire program it should be emphasized at each meeting that the individuals involved have complete responsibility for their part in the program and will be evaluated on their ability to carry out their self-established goals.

If top management reiterates this policy at *each* meeting, lower-level managers will be extremely reluctant to risk embarrassment in front of their peers, to say nothing of possibly jeopardizing future status within the organization, by failing to meet goals. However, in the event that one or more of the members should attempt to present excuses for falling behind schedule, it is important that the chief executive or other top management not fall into the trap of reprimanding the person or expressing disappointment at his or her nonperformance. To do so would imply taking the responsibility off the manager's back. Instead, a simple statement like "Sorry to hear that, Joe. You're aware, of course, that this is *your* project. Now, what are you going to do to alleviate these problems?" will almost always get the project back on the track again.

Once the program has been completed, a performance review should be conducted for all employees involved, together with a thorough analysis of the program's results. This can set the stage for a new program to be developed in the same manner.

PROGRAM BENEFITS

The program *will work.* The potential advantages for organizations that are willing to take the time and trouble to implement a program of this type are so obvious that I sometimes wonder why everyone isn't using it. To name a few:

1. Assured Results through Accountability represents a programmed road map built around real data and facts such as due dates, percentages, and dollar volume. This brings results.
2. Because the program is based on individual accountability, it gives the chief executive the opportunity to utilize time more effectively on more important areas of the business.
3. It provides the opportunity to check real progress continuously, in total, or by division specifically, as required.

In addition to the immediate rewards provided by a positive management approach, there are several long-range benefits that will almost certainly be acquired.

1. The program encourages sound decision making at all levels.
2. It develops and forces a closer understanding of problem solving through better communications between executives and subordinates.
3. It furnishes a clearer understanding of individual action as a part of group action.
4. It provides an unusual vehicle for developing greater individual achievement and gives an incentive for this achievement.
5. It provides the logical, sound basis for an integrated management-by-direction program.

6. It provides guided direction aimed at upgrading executive performance from fair to good and from good to outstanding.
7. It forms stepping stones to long-range planning.

YES, THERE CAN BE PROBLEMS

It should be obvious at this time that the step-by-step program outlined in this chapter is based primarily on a strong code of managerial accountability. There is no built-in mechanism for failure. Because of this, it is important that the goals and projects agreed upon are achievable. The program cannot function if top management, in its zeal to acquire maximum results within the shortest possible time span, allows itself to be trapped into approving impossible standards based on wishful thinking or blue-sky expectations.

With this in mind, I'd like to close this chapter by being completely candid and sharing with you some of the errors and blunders I have made in installing earlier programs of this type, in the hope that you will not have to experience them yourself.

1. Since Assuring Results through Accountability is a continuing effort, do not allow your subordinates' goals to be too difficult the first time around. Most managers will set their goals too high. It is very important that your subordinates succeed on the first go-around. It must, however, be a challenge.
2. Do not allow everyday responsibilities and requirements to enter into goal or project development.
3. Do not allow any individual manager to have too many projects.
4. Be certain that each manager thinks through his or her project thoroughly and completely. Be sure not only that all the manager's subordinates are involved, but that they program their own subprojects. A chain is only as strong as its weakest link.
5. If there are too many goals, be certain to eliminate unnecessary ones. It is better to accomplish a few more important goals than to partially accomplish many.
6. Last, but most important: As long as the employee determined the goal, how it was to be accomplished, what the end result would be, and in what period of time it would be completed, be

firm in the policy that you have every right to expect the end result that was initially established. *No excuses.* The participants are expected to provide for contingencies!

The program outlined in the preceding pages involves a little more time and effort than the typical planning programs used by most companies. However, on the basis of my observations over the years, I can safely say that 80 percent of the other long- and short-range plans I have seen never accomplish their intended objective. This is because of two factors: (1) management fails to take the time and trouble to make a thorough management inventory, and (2) the program lacks a practical method to ensure that the goals will be met.

With the ever-increasing proliferation of management jobs in American industry, accountability is an ingredient that is not only necessary but virtually mandatory if an organization is to survive. The companies who have recognized this and done something about it are the ones who are around today to brag about it. It is the companies that will do something about it in the years ahead that will be paying dividends to their stockholders in the future.

6

Putting Direction in the Board of Directors

Dreadful things are just as apt to happen when unknowledgeable people control a situation as when ill-natured people are in charge.

Don Marquis

The role of the corporate director has in most instances remained virtually unchanged since the turn of the century. Despite the increasing tempo of operations and growing specialization brought about by quantum jumps in industrial technology, the corporate director is too often only a figurehead, duly listening as corporate policy is enunciated and nodding on appropriate cue. His official duties consume four or five hours of meeting time each month or quarter, for which he is charitably rewarded. Overall performance is graded primarily on attendance records.

The ritual is repeated with monotonous regularity for the purpose of reassuring company management that it enjoys the confidence and support of the panel that ostensibly represents the company owners. The really important factors, however, are normally the prestige and vanity of the directors themselves, many of whom do not represent or serve the owners or, for that matter, anyone but themselves.

A major contributing factor to this alarming condition is the fact that many board memberships are awarded for the wrong reasons. Appointment to a board is often contingent upon personal friendships or the desire to lend the board an air of respectability, rather than on ability to perform. In some instances this may be a calculated device to load the board with individuals who are reluctant to make waves. More often, however, it is based on a failure to recognize the full extent of a board member's potential impact on the organization.

State laws of incorporation normally confer broad powers upon directors. They may declare dividends; approve policy matters such as mergers and acquisitions; establish policy concerning audits, financing, and general expenditures; change corporate bylaws; select operating managers; establish executive salaries; and perform many other important functions. Yet despite these inherent powers many boards today, by the most charitable definition, are mediocre bodies that resemble arid deserts of untapped talents, unfulfilled capabilities, and misplaced hopes.

In fairness to the people who, in good faith, agree to serve on these boards, it must be stated that in many instances the lethargy evidenced by many board members is not of their own choosing. It is caused primarily by the procedure through which most boards are selected. In too many cases the job of being a director is incidental to the primary vocation of the individual concerned. Often people are placed on the board simply because their names lend prestige to a company.

In a staff report put out by the Judiciary Committee of the House of Representatives, a tabulation was prepared concerning the status of directors serving at 74 leading companies. Within these 74 companies, 146 directors served on 20 or more boards, 228 served on 15 or more, and 307 on 10 or more!

For the people in these positions to fulfill their obligations for any one of the companies they represent, to say nothing of taking care of the needs of their own business or profession, comes as close to an exercise in futility as trying to bail water with a sieve. To further hamper their performance, there is frequently a tacit agreement between top management and the board that board members will function only as figureheads. Often this occurs when strong or dominant presidents feel that they have all the answers and resist outside interference, or when a company is run by a family or selfish interests who are willing to sacrifice efficiency of operation for corporate domination.

In either event, the end result was summed up eloquently by Martin Stone, chief executive officer of Monogram Industries, who stated in an article published by *Business Week*, May 22, 1981, "Too many directors are not in a position to learn enough about a company to serve responsibly. At best they acquire a smattering of knowledge and become only a mild irritant and an occasional nuisance."

In recent years some efforts have been made to strengthen the usefulness of the board. Most of these have proved palliative only; others are even contradictory. Some corporations rely exclusively on an "inside board" composed entirely of the firm's management. In theory, at least, the inside director brings an intimate knowledge of company operations to board meetings. The built-in problem here is whether an organization can expect true independence or objectivity from a board member who is hired, promoted, appraised, and rewarded by existing managemnt. As one inside board member put it, "It's difficult to generate any wild enthusiasm among inside board members over challenging a proposal that has just been advanced by the man who pays your salary." Also, an inside board composed of members representing diverse portions of an organization may frequently be prone to lobbying for items that serve their individual interests, rather than representing the company as a whole.

In an effort to ensure a balance of power, some companies have opted for a compromise arrangement where the board is made up of both inside and outside members. Unfortunately, this too often generates some king-sized problems. The major difficulty is that boards of this type tend to be dominated by insiders who are closer to the pulse of the operation and are admittedly more knowledgeable concerning its problems and needs.

An alternate but little-used variation of the mixed board consists of a top tier of outside directors and employee representatives and a lower tier of inside management employees. The top tier outranks the lower tier and, in effect, supervises the company's supervisors. In theory this ensures that inside directors do not dominate the board. Performance records on two-tiered board membership tend to be sketchy. The best statistics on this come from West Germany, where the practice has been prevalent for many years. According to recent reports it has not been an overwhelming success. In fact, many West German corporations are now reverting to more conventional methods.

Within the past five years a new and somewhat controversial type of board member has emerged on the corporate scene. The practice consists of appointing to the board one or more members from the hierarchy of labor organizations. The first major company to do his was Chrysler Corporation, when back in 1980 it included retired UAW president Douglas A. Frazer. Since then Western Air Lines, Pan American Airlines, Eastern Airlines, and others have followed this trend.

Up till now the concept has not been a smashing success and has received somewhat mixed reviews from both sides of the corporate aisle. Many management-oriented board members feel uncomfortable with the idea of sharing authority with employee representatives. Conversely, some unions have voiced a fear that workers may see little need for a union if they are represented in corporate board rooms.

The basic fault with all these methods is that they fail to come to grips with the real problem: how to obtain knowledgeable people who will devote a sufficient amount of time to make a significant contribution to the operation. A contributing factor to the general impotence of the board of directors seems to be the aura of mystery that usually enshrouds board membership. Little known, half-understood, often held in awe by those below the policy-making level, "The Board" is often regarded as a corporate supreme court that is above reproach and therefore an unlikely target for reform.

In recent years, however, there appears to be a growing tendency on the part of the courts and the stockholders themselves to demand more personal liability from board members. The firing by the government of most of the directors of Continental Illinois Bank was a humbling experience for them and has predictably caused some potential and existing directors to give serious thought to weighing the advantages and disadvantages of board membership.

In an era when American business is beginning to rely more and more on a strict code of accountability, it was perhaps inevitable that some new methods would be devised to upgrade the performance of the board of directors to a level where it is better able to cope with the problems of modern industry. The changes have come about primarily during the past decade, and they were motivated by the realities of increased legal responsibility and perhaps a sincere desire to put to rest the clearly outmoded "buddy system" of a bygone era.

THE COMMITTEE-ORIENTED BOARD

Many of today's larger companies are rapidly reverting to a committee-oriented board composed of members who represent diverse backgrounds, some of whom might even have acquired their expertise outside the world of business. A board of this type requires a keen sense of balance to ensure that members of individual committees are better equipped than the board as a whole to deal effectively with issues regarding their particular area of expertise. These committees will vary from one company to another, depending on individual needs. A board may contain an audit committee, an executive committee, a finance committee, a legal affairs committee, a compensation and pension committee, a personnel management committee, and so on.

The most common of these is the audit committee, whose members will probably have a long varied background in finance or general management. A member of an audit committee is almost always an outsider who often will sit on several other boards in the same capacity. He or she should be independent of management and free from any relationship that could interfere with independent judgment. Ideally, the audit committee should have the power to direct and supervise an investigation into any matter brought to its attention, including the right to retain outside counsel in connection with an investigation. In the light of some recent corporate improprieties, the need for such an entity is obvious—so obvious, in fact, that since June 1978 a policy of the New York Stock Exchange requires that all domestic, publicly owned companies listing securities on the New York Stock Exchange must, as a condition of listing, establish an audit committee composed of members independent from the board of directors.

Another area of specialization by the board of directors in many companies is a public responsibility committee, sometimes alternately referred to as a public issues committee, a corporate responsibility committee, or a people resource committee. The need for a specialized group of this type has been generated, for the most part, by increased emphasis on social issues that affect a company. These could include adverse media publicity, environmental problems, affirmative action lawsuits, consumer boycotts, employee benefits, and other problems that would tend to usurp a large portion of the time and effort by the full board but could be turned over to a committee of four or five members who are particularly skilled in these areas. Members of a public responsibility committee may be either inside or outside members, but they are usually outsiders, some of whom may not be strong in actual business experience but possess a background in things like sociology or public opinion analysis.

On the basis of this type of expertise the public responsibility committee can initiate independent investigations and subsequently make recommendations to the full board based on competent analysis of the issues involved. The public responsibility committee, as a tool for upgrading the effectiveness and efficiency of the board, is used by many large corporations, including Sears Roebuck, General Electric, American Telephone & Telegraph, Dow Chemical, General Mills, and many other blue-chip companies listed in the *Fortune* 500.

The committee concept has caught on exceedingly well in recent years and has been a large factor in obviating what in the past was frequently a hodgepodge of widely diversified opinions from members who had little knowledge of specific issues.

One company that has had considerable success with the committee-oriented board is the Connecticut General Insurance Corporation of Hartford. In addition to an audit committee, Connecticut General retains on the board several other committees, all of which are comprised of individuals who possess expertise in the areas to which they are assigned. Among the committees maintained by the board at Connecticut General are:

1. A *financial resources committee*, whose purpose is to meet approximately every other month and report to the board on the management of the corporation's financial resources. Its activities include review of the adequacy of capital resources and inquiry into current and planned utilization of capital and the corresponding risk/reward relationships. Additionally, the financial resources committee is responsible for reviewing and reporting on management's recommendations concerning dividend payments to stockholders; changes in the corporation's capital structure; divestment, diversification, or acquisition; bank lines of credit; and other matters involving the commitment of financial resources on which board approval is sought.

2. An *investment committee*, whose purpose is to meet twice a month to review and report to the board on the management of the investments of the company and its subsidiaries. It is the function of this committee to assure itself and the board that investments are being managed prudently and effectively. This committee reviews and approves investment policies, investment guidelines, and schedules of authority for making investment decisions. It also periodically examines the processes used to ensure that these policies, guidelines, and schedules are being followed.

3. A *committee on directors*, which meets once each year and at such other times as might be necessary to assure itself and the board, through appropriate inquiry and review, that the chairman of the board is effectively managing the development and maintenance of the board's membership and organization. To accomplish this, the committee inquires into the work of the chairman of the board in this area to whatever depth is necessary and reports to the board as a whole.

Greater participation by the board in an era when corporate dealings are becoming increasingly complex is clearly long past due. The increasing use of the committee-oriented board has resulted in a marked improvement from the conventional board, which, unfortunately, is still widely used, particularly in smaller companies.

The committee-oriented board functions best in larger corporations that have numerous specialized problems and the financial ability to acquire the multifaceted expertise that is required from widely diversified sources. For smaller and medium-sized companies, however, there is an alternative that is rapidly becoming integrated into the American business system. This involves retaining a working, or professional, director as a member of the board.

THE WORKING DIRECTOR

Admittedly, the working director has not yet developed into a mandatory requirement in America's corporate structure. Nevertheless, the need for some new type of board member in smaller and medium-sized companies has reached a point where many corporations are taking a long, hard look at the advantages and disadvantages of acquiring such a professional.

The concept of the working director can be briefly stated. The company elects to its board a director whose responsibility is one of deeper involvement than that of the other members. This person spends a substantial amount of time each month on the job, becoming very familiar with the company, its personnel, its operating methods, and its prospects. As an outsider, such a director brings to the company an indispensable element—objectivity. As an adopted insider, she or he enjoys the voting rights, privileges, obligations, and burdens of board membership. This director's duties are to probe, to question, to advise. If he or she discharges these responsibilities conscientiously and with competence, this individual can make the board of directors—and the company—vastly more effective and profitable.

Although the operation differs somewhat in principle, the concept of the working director probably originated in Great Britain, where a member of the board frequently also functions as a company manager and where only nominal distinctions exist between directors, managers, and executives.

According to a survey conducted by the Institute of Directors in London, 67 percent of its members describe their work as being predominantly that of a general manager. Only 10 percent of those queried regarded themselves as "whole-time directors." This tends to support the theory that British business is run to a large degree by professional managers and executives. An interesting sidelight to this is that British board members also tend to confine their director-ships to fewer companies. Only 20 percent of them hold two or more directorships and only relatively few are members of several boards.

Working directors in America, while functioning somewhat differently from their overseas cousins, first appeared informally on the industrial scene some years back and probably evolved from the favorable results that were achieved when a particular board member decided to assume duties and responsibilities far in excess of what was actually expected.

A More Professional Member

In contrast to both their inside and outside contemporaries, working directors in America are retained as professionals—paid to do the director's job, and even something more. With the blessing of the chief executive officer, the working director peeks and probes and performs in areas where an outside board member would not nor-mally be welcome. On the other hand, directors do not execute pol-icy. Instead they work and get results *through other people*. Ideally this keeps them from becoming bogged down in administrative de-tails, and it obviates accusations of meddling in operating routines.

The advantages of retaining a working director, as opposed to a conventional director, can best by summed up by listing the duties, responsibilities, and limitations that go with the job.

1. *The working director brings a fresh viewpoint to the board.* The viewpoint of the working director differs from that of the conven-tional director by an entire dimension. Typical outside directors may admittedly possess open minds and an uncompromised attitude. Nevertheless, they can act only on facts that are presented to them by insiders. Their decisions are therefore only as good as the infor-mation that they are spoon-fed. Working directors do not rely solely on "official" sources for their information. They initiate inquiries and conduct forays of their own. Outside directors, even if they took the trouble to explore on their own, would scarcely be in a posi-tion to follow through effectively.

2. *The working director pinpoints problems before they erupt.* The working director is a familiar figure who pops in and out at will and who speaks to (but does not give orders to) corporate personnel at all levels. Because of this he or she has an opportunity to prescribe preventive medicine that may obviate ultimate surgery. Addition-

ally, this director can be of particular help in the field of his or her own special competence, such as finance, labor relations, work measurement, or personnel.

3. *The working director concentrates on policy making and whether personnel apply policies wisely to existing operations.* Because of this, the director is in an extremely favorable position to advise both the chief executive and the board on policy matters and personnel problems.

4. *The working director contributes experience, knowledge, know-how, and contacts from many diverse sources.* Unlike the conventional director, he or she has a background that is rich in many different disciplines. The working director is familiar with the mores of many management professions and acquainted with the problems and prospects of entire industries. Except for the most gifted people, inside directors are severely handicapped when unfamiliar problems are encountered, such as diversification or acquisitions. A working director is equipped to rise above these limitations. The factors necessary to sound business practice, fortunately, are so nearly uniform that a working director can function effectively in several unrelated industries. In fact there are often advantages to analyzing one business in the light of others.

5. *The working director stimulates the president and other top-echelon executives to better performance.* By virtue of his or her office, the working director works closely with the chief executive and other top-level executives, serving as a confidential advisor, idea source, and sounding board. He or she may also, on occasion, act as the devil's advocate to the top company officers.

6. *The working director's position assures that his or her voice will be heard.* Middle managers reporting to the board are normally bound by propriety and self-interest to lobby for their points of view with the utmost subtlety. Outside consultants must sell their ideas to the board. The working director, however, speaks as a peer among peers and cannot be misquoted. His or her views are treated with respect. What's more impressive, the working director has a vote to back them up. In short, continuity of relationship permits the working director to assume responsibility for results.

Organizational Relationships

To be truly effective, the working director should always be selected by the board's dominant or controlling group. Consequently, he or she represents the company's governing faction and in a sense helps keep it in control. At first glance this may not seem entirely desirable or even advisable. "Where then," we might ask, "is this director's independence?"

In practice, however, the working director puts his or her objectivity at the disposal of those in charge. To do otherwise would place the working director in a functional vacuum—or even worse, pit him or her against the majority. Actually, the fact that the working director is selected by the controlling group should cause no raised eyebrows. After all, this is the identical route by which the conventional director arrives on the scene. All that differs is the mode of operation.

The working director must work closely, even intimately, with the company's chief executive officer. It is the president's word, after all, that opens doors to the working director and gives her or him carte blanche to peek, probe, and perform. This type of close relationship will vastly multiply the director's effectiveness. Because of this special and perhaps unique relationship, some properties must be observed. The president, for example, must provide the working director with the same operating and financial data that the principle executives receive.

The director should never initiate an investigation without informing the president of all findings. Suggestions and recommendations acquired as a result of these investigations must be brought to the attention of the president and no other executive. To be completely effective, a working director should always take a stand on an issue. He or she should never avoid a decision even when this decision conflicts with that of the chief executive officer.

In spite of the right to dig through the corporate structure, talk to lower-echelon personnel, and examine existing procedures, it should be emphasized that the working director functions on the policy level only. Because of this unique status, selection of an individual who can successfully fit into this critical role can sometimes be difficult. If the wrong person is selected, the problems that are generated can often outweigh the benefits derived.

Criteria for Selection

A basic qualification for the successful working director is that the person selected be more concerned with managerial behavior than personality. Since the director must get results through other people, she or he cannot afford to indulge in personal grudges or become actively involved in departmental feuds. Instead, the director's role should be more like a catalyst between operating management and the board of directors. In this capacity she or he can act as a motivating force, helping officers and key personnel to establish their own goals.

In companies where a working director has acted as a viable addition to the staff, the three most important ingredients for this position were:

1. The ability to arouse the enthusiasm of officers and key personnel.

2. The ability to stay in the background and allow executives to receive full credit for their results.

3. The ability to differentiate between the important and the unimportant. The person who swats at flies while standing in a pit full of crocodiles is clearly out of depth in a position of this type.

A special type of climate is required to make a working directorship succeed. First, the director must possess unique qualities of personality, character, and experience. He or she must have an analytical mind, a sound business background, an ability to work with and through people, a willingness to needle top executives into self-examination, a flexible attitude that adapts to different corporations and industries, and, finally, a willingness to forego praise and credit in deference to the operating managers.

The company must possess certain characteristics, too. Among them, its president must be willing to accept criticism, must agree to identify problems, and must admit that corporate performance can always be improved. The president must be willing to act on recommendations advanced by the working director.

Establishing this unique brand of rapport is not always easy. The director may even find that it is not always advisable to accept offers of directorships. In one instance, for example, a working director rejected a seat on the board of a company with sales of $20,000,000. The business was highly successful, sales were at unprecedented levels, profits were strong, and the outlook unclouded. There was just one problem. The president's self-confidence was pitched so high that others could no longer get through. Under these circumstances the working director would have been as functionless as snowshoes in August. In another case a directorship was rejected because management would not accept the principle of unfettered inquiry. Under such conditions a working director can offer little more than any other member of the board—that is, a judgment based on penetrating questions posed at board meetings. On the other hand, with the necessary support, a working director can accomplish much more than lies within the scope of the conventional board member. A single example will suggest the possibilities.

A corporation that had entered the fiscal year $750,000 in the red appointed a working director out of desperation. The person selected for the job went to work on a full-time basis, conducting a detailed and comprehensive study of all facets of the business. His analysis of company facts and figures disclosed that loose wage rates had been permitted to develop over a period of years, but the changes had been so gradual and so subtle that neither management nor the board of directors had been aware of the size of the problem—or if they were aware they ignored it. The working director then assumed the task of explaining the situation to union officials and was eventually able to sell them a new and more realistic wage plan. Once this was adopted the company moved back into the black ink and stayed there.

Since the working director is a relatively new type of professional, there is no clearinghouse for candidates. However, a potential pool of competent working directors is being created out of the increasing number of executives who are retiring from their companies at age 65 or earlier. Because of the difference in individual performance, one would hesitate to make a flat statement on the amount of experience required for this position. Nevertheless, it is hard to conceive that anyone would be completely qualified with less than 25 years of experience in business management.

Concerning compensation, ordinarily the working director should be paid a retainer instead of an amount per meeting or per diem. There are several reasons for this arrangement. First, the working director cannot predict his or her working schedule. The amount of time devoted to a company, like the time a physician gives to a patient, is determined by the characteristics of the case. Also, there is a psychological factor. Under a retainer system, the working director is greeted with pleasure when he or she arrives at the company and begins to work. Under any other arrangement, the director is not welcome because each arrival signals that the meter is running and a fee will be charged.

Finally, by working on a retainer basis, a working director achieves the financial independence that nurtures an objective point of view and does not compromise professional status.

Problems and Pitfalls

While the addition of a working director to any corporate board will, under normal conditions, vastly enhance the effectiveness of that body, there are some problems that can develop, particularly if the wrong person is chosen or if conditions exist that will inhibit the director's performance.

To expect the director to perform miracles overnight or under next-to-impossible conditions is completely unrealistic. As with most managerial tasks, the results attained will be contingent to a large degree on support received from top management and the degree of authority under which the director is permitted to operate.

Here are some basic guidelines that should influence a company's decision about whether or not to retain a working director.

1. *Working directors function best in medium-sized companies.* The reason for this is obvious. Larger corporations generally employ teams of internal consultants who, at considerably higher cost, can perform many of the working director's duties. However, such consultants have neither the strong voice in policy nor the close association with the president that is enjoyed by the professional director. Another limitation posed by a large corporation is geography. A company that has widely scattered branches does not lend itself to conscientious grass-roots study.

2. *The working director succeeds only where he or she is wanted.* When a company is negative toward the idea of having a working director, there is little hope for success. For example, in one company the president was clearly an egomaniac. His overbearing personality stifled the initiative of subordinates and directors alike. Worse yet, he could not tolerate criticism of the mildest kind. A working director in this organization would have been worse than useless.

Grudging acquiescence and half-hearted cooperation can also be fatal. Genuine enthusiasm, of course, is the ideal requisite. Realistically, however, this emotion is quite rare. Second-best is an attitude of enlightened neutrality and a willingness to give the system an honest test.

3. *The working director's task requires great delicacy to be executed in an effective manner.* Unquestionably, the director must be tactful and sincere. The director must assure by word, deed, and manner that he or she is not an inquisitor bent on unearthing scandal or incompetency. Gaining the cooperation of lower-echelon executives is a tedious task. It takes considerable diplomacy to convince all levels that the working director seeks neither glory nor gain but works only to upgrade efficiency and boost profits. Laying this groundwork can be time-consuming and requires patience and persistence.

Checklist for the Working Director

Unfortunately, the role of the working director has not yet been fully accepted by American industry. Part of this is probably due to a perverse reluctance on the part of many businesspeople to accept change. From a purely objective standpoint, some of the reluctance may be justified. After all, in too many instances there are no clear-cut criteria for what a conventional director is supposed to do, and any attempt to further complicate the role of this corporate entity may often be regarded as even further entangling what is already an industrial can of worms.

Nevertheless, a simple look at the areas of usefulness of the average conventional board member as opposed to the potential function of a working director leaves little doubt concerning the need for a person of this type in most organizations. If further proof is needed to support this statement, consider the following checklist prepared specifically for use by a working director and then ask yourself how many of these areas could be effectively probed by a typical member of a conventional board.

Does management operate on a planned and controlled basis, and does it formulate its plans and policies on the basis of adequate factual material and careful study?

1. Are plans predicated on factual information?
2. Is there any long-range plan to improve the firm's position in the market?
3. Has anybody ever set down on paper a five-year forecast of financial resources and requirements?

4. Is there a long-range plan of product development?
5. Is there a plan for replacement of physical facilities or personnel?
6. Are existing plans predicated on factual information?

Have the company's sales policies and efforts improved and will they continue to improve?

1. Is the company improving or at least maintaining its position in the industry?
2. Is the industry growing, declining, or static?
3. Is management aware of long-term economic trends within the industry?
4. Is the product line properly designed?
5. Does the product line fit today's market?
6. What is the relationship of the replacement market to the whole?
7. To what extent has the market been abnormally expanded in the past ten years?
8. What is the effect of competitive conditions on normal sales?
9. Is the line designed in such a manner that there are a maximum number of interchangeable parts?
10. Has the line gained or lost customers? Why?
11. Is the line sufficiently diversified?
12. Is the line designed for low production cost?
13. Are sales territories too large or too small?
14. Have sales territories been changed to meet population and buying-power shifts?
15. Do salespeople have adequate incentive?
16. Are salespeople trained to meet the demands of the future?
17. Are the company's prices competitive?
18. Has the company spent enough for promotion?
19. Are present promotion policies effective?
20. Has the sales management inventoried its customers, actual and potential?

Do company facilities and operating methods allow it to compete effectively and profitably?

1. Are production and inventory control operating properly?
2. Are inventories excessive? If so, why?
3. Are inventories adequate to give good service to customers?
4. Does management know what its break-even point is?
5. Does management know what to do if sales should drop off sharply?
6. Does management know what to do and what the results would be if a sizable number of orders were suddenly canceled?
7. Does management attempt to budget each executive and supervisor in such a manner that he or she can operate within predetermined limits?
8. Is cost accounting up to date?
9. Is cost accounting meaningful?
10. Is cost accounting used as a tool of control?
11. Is the financial or control department equal to other departments or is it regarded as "those damn bookkeepers"?
12. Can the company compete effectively in production?
13. Is equipment modern and efficient?
14. Is equipment in balance?
15. Is equipment utilized to maximum capacity?
16. Do production delays and inefficiencies result in excessive downtime or setup time?
17. Have standards been maintained?
18. Is the wage incentive effective or has it deteriorated?
19. Have guaranteed wage rates crept in to destroy incentive and control, resulting in excessive labor costs?

Does management operate on a planned and controlled basis and does it formulate its plans and policies on the basis of factual material and careful study?

1. Does each executive know his or her place on the team?

2. Are major functions such as production, sales, personnel, finance, and engineering properly balanced?

3. Does top management make all the decisions, or is it creating a climate for decision making among the lower echelon in the belief that this is the proper way for managers to develop?

4. Is each major function managed by a competent person, qualified by education, experience, and temperament?

5. If each functional manager does not have one or more potential successors, what needs to be done to develop this succession?

6. Are lines of authority and responsibility clearly defined?

7. Is the organization a harmonious group, or are there those whose self-interests transcend the interest of the management team?

Even a superficial review of the possible areas for improvement that are contained in this checklist will dramatically point up how a working director, endowed with the proper qualifications and authority, can function in situations where a conventional board member would be completely lost. Whether any single individual could function at 100 percent efficiency in all these areas is, of course, highly doubtful. Being human beings, working directors have their limitations. But if they are honest they will admit their shortcomings when they are unable to define problems or offer solutions and will recommend the necessary procedures to fill the gaps.

In the meantime, corporate management, particularly in smaller and medium-sized companies, needs to wake up to the fact that the wheels of change are grinding and the clock is ticking. A good, effective board of directors is one of management's strongest assets. It is too important to be allowed to die of obsolescence.

Establishing Rapport with Subordinates

The art of dealing with people is the foremost secret of successful men. A man's success in handling people is the very yardstick by which the outcome of his whole life's work is measured.

Paul Parker

Historically, the relationship between labor and management has been largely adversary and marked with general suspicion and short-sighted animosity. Thankfully, the goon-squad tactics of a previous era have yielded somewhat to practices like collective bargaining, arbitration, and grievance procedures. Yet an honest appraisal points up the fact that labor and management, in most companies, still regard each other with a smoldering hostility that stems from a colossal lack of understanding and a marked shortage of cooperation by both parties.

Labor's fear of being victimized by unfair management practices is a constant and continual sentiment. Management's suspicion of all labor demands is often a built-in negative factor that divides the two groups into opposing enemy camps. In union shops the hostility surfaces in confrontations at grievance hearings or at the bargaining table. In nonunion shops management frequently lives in fear—sometimes approaching paranoia—that workers might become organized.

It is high time that management took the initiative and stopped reacting negatively to what others set in motion. In many companies today, what passes for an employee relations policy is nothing more than a defensive reaction to forces initiated by others. It took several decades for management to realize that its power was not a God-given right, but a privilege it maintained simply because labor was too weak to reach out and take some of the things that should logically have been its prerogatives.

When labor first began to flex its muscles, many of its demands appeared futile, if not downright amusing. Nevertheless, labor demanded a ten-hour day and got it despite screams of rage that went up from management. There were more screams when labor demanded, and got, an eight-hour day. Now, with management's screams somewhat muffled, some industries already have a 30- to 35-hour week, plus other benefits too numerous to mention. During the past several decades labor has done more than improve its lot. It has become the dominant force in American industry.

In addition to the pressues exerted by organized labor, industry must now comply with many laws on the federal and state books controlling practices like hiring, firing, work rules, wage rates, discipline, hours of work, pensions, insurance, and seniority. To their credit, the managers of many organizations have attempted to live with these laws and have even made progress in orchestrating a better relationship with employees and labor unions. Unfortunately, it is difficult to orchestrate when an entity like big government is holding the baton.

Laws, of course, can be changed or made inactive by other laws or amendments. But this takes time—and doing. It's a matter of record that it is easier to get a law on the books than to take it off. It is also infinitely easier to get a clause into a union contract than to get it out. Labor found, in many cases, that trying to change existing laws is time-consuming and very expensive. Management, because it is usually regarded as the "heavy" in this scenario, has found it even more difficult.

If we're ready to accept the assumption that the legal status quo changes very slowly, if at all, the logical question that follows is: What can management do within the framework of existing laws to maintain some semblance of its rights and at the same time ensure a degree of empathy with the workers who produce its products and services?

To answer this question, it is first necessary to pose several additional questions. For example, can management really blame present conditions on the "big, bad unions"? Or on that crowd back in Washington? Has industry really been taken for a sleigh ride by outside forces? Or is it just possible that management itself willingly relinquished the reins of leadership because it was too apathetic or naive to cope with the opposing forces under their own ground rules?

What, for example, was management doing while organized labor was taking over the store? Did the majority of our industrial leaders ever make a serious effort to assess the real needs of the American worker? Has management, for the most part, ever attempted to create a climate where employees could take problems to their supervisors, instead of a shop steward or union officer? Just what *was* management doing while organized labor was moving into the driver's seat?

The answer to this, sad to state, is "surprisingly little," except to maintain a conspiracy of silence at this "upstart group," hoping it would die off and go away.

It should now be obvious to everyone that organized labor isn't going to go away. Nor is it going to easily relinquish the gains it has made during the past 40 years. Why should it? Labor's tactics have been extremely effective—so effective that we might well ask why management hasn't thought of coping with the situation by applying the same general principles. Think about this for a moment: Is there anything that organized labor is doing that management couldn't do just as well?

WHAT DOES THE UNION OFFER?

Reduced to a simple sentence, this is the situation: Organized labor has found a king-sized niche in the American business system because it provides what management has failed to provide.

Shop stewards, for example, retain their present role because they have supplemented what the supervisors should be providing. Stewards are in business because they are able to convince employees that they have the employees' interests at heart. If management, including supervision, possessed this single trait, worker effectiveness and productivity would be sharply increased.

Let's take an analytical look at exactly what the union offers to its members and those who might wish to become members.

1. It pledges wage increases, more benefits, and better working conditions. And it usually comes through with enough improvements to keep the membership quiet.

2. The union keeps its members posted. The information may be union-slanted and perhaps even a bit inaccurate, but at least the union talks. It *says something*. Management usually says nothing at all, or says very little.

3. The union goes to bat for a member. It gets action on a grievance. When union members have gripes, they usually go to the stewards rather than to their supervisors. Why? Because they can generally get some action out of the stewards.

4. Union membership gives people a chance to participate. They can take part in union affairs and can run for office. They're not just numbers on time cards. He's Brother Jones; she's Sister Smith.

5. The union offers social activity: beer and bingo for workers and their spouses and fun for their kids. The hall is a gathering place where workers feel at home.

6. The union treats its members as people. They are visited in the hospital, are helped with roof repairs, and are on the receiving

end of a number of acts of personal aid and attention. This makes them feel good.

Read these benefits offered by the union again. Then ask yourself, Would it not be possible for management to perform most of these functions as well as or better than the officials who represent the union? There is little need to state here that few managers have attempted to do this. Assuming that managers truly have the interests of their employees at heart, as many managers claim they do, they've done a bad job of convincing their employees of this fact.

The problem is obviously one of misunderstanding, born of poor or insincere communications. Management, through this entire era of growing crisis, has maintained a stoic silence about itself. Meanwhile, its detractors have hacked away at it, weakening its very foundations, and management has said nothing. It's getting awfully late!

Managers must take some positive steps to bridge the awesome empathy gap that currently exists between themselves and the people they employ. Let's consider some of the things that management could do to improve its image and simultaneously help itself regain its right to manage.

LABOR–MANAGEMENT NEGOTIATIONS

A typical collective bargaining session can be historically compared to the seal show at a three-ring circus. Back in the early days of labor–management negotiations, the scenario consisted of management assuming the role of the ringmaster, with labor representatives playing the part of the trained seals. The act consisted of the ringmaster barking several times, after which the seals would bark back. With these preliminaries out of the way, the ringmaster would then throw the seals a fish. After a half-century of these theatrics the analogy is still valid. There has been one minor change: in today's collective bargaining session it is labor that plays the role of the ringmaster.

This role reversal did not come about through Darwin's theory of evolution. It occurred because management permitted it to occur. Throughout the years management has continued to operate on a policy it formulated back in the early days of labor–management negotiations when concessions were made unilaterally by management simply because management was the only group that had anything to give.

This concept is, of course, no longer valid. Yet management, for the most part, has failed to wake up and smell the coffee. It has convinced both the union and the employees that it is a ruthless tight-fisted entity that can be induced to make concessions only by tremendous pressure exerted by financially well heeled groups. It's admittedly a little late for management in organized shops to exclude unions from the industrial scene. I'm not sure this would even be beneficial. Nevertheless, management must get the message across that gains in pay and fringe benefits must be geared to corresponding gains in productivity. Both workers and the unions that represent them must be made to realize that the best way to improve their lot under our current economic system is to produce more goods and services, rather than periodically intimidating industry with blue-sky demands.

I recall an incident that occurred a few years ago at a parts assembly plant in the Midwest where we were called in after the company had been encountering severe financial setbacks. An investigation on of the company's history showed that the firm had originated in the founder's basement, but it had grown to a status of six plants and 375 employees with $6 million in annual sales. This growth had been achieved through a policy of quality production, close management vigilance over costs, and piecework rates high enough to offer a real incentive to workers yet low enough to be sound and economical.

Then came a period when changes such as increased competition and new technology began to slacken management's grip. Shortly afterward a union stepped in and pressured for changes in the piecework rate structure. Within months the entire piecework pattern swerved off course. Costs began to surge, productivity slackened, and the company began wallowing in the pool of red ink. Matching the union's pressure for bigger pay boosts was the sales department's demand for an end to price increases. The ultimate result was that quality control fell apart, work methods degenerated, and the work flow deteriorated into a state of utter confusion.

A comprehensive study revealed the fact that for the company to remain solvent it would be necessary, among other things, to discard the present piecework system and install a standard hourly incentive plan geared to obtaining a fair day's production for a day's pay, commensurate with other companies in the same industry.

Management accepted this proposal readily but the union was adamant in its demand for retention of status quo. To cope with this we worked up, with the assistance of company management, a presentation designed to give graphic evidence to union officials that if the employees gave full cooperation, wage levels could be maintained and might even be increased. It was made clear through presentation of irrefutable facts and figures that the alternate choice, rejection of the program, would endanger the company's very existence and the existence of the workers' jobs.

It was then explained that the proposal, which included job evaluation, supervisor training, work scheduling, work-flow changes, and work simplification, would be implemented with the assistance of union officials and key employees, who would be free to make proposals and suggestions relative to the program's development.

After some minor modification, the proposal was accepted by the union and subsequently agreed to in a vote by the union's membership. To assist in selling the program to the workers, we took the trouble to draft a comprehensive letter, which was sent to each employee, that outlined in detail the aims and benefits that would be acquired by the modified procedure.

The story has a happy ending. The initial projected company savings of $100,000 annually actually turned out to be a conservative estimate. Labor costs were reduced by 12 percent. Average take-home pay for employees was actually increased. And the company is now operating on the black side of the ledger. Moreover, I have it on the word of company management that since the program has been placed into effect there has been a remarkably improved spirit of cooperation between management and union officials.

This program succeeded, in my opinion, because primarily both the union and the employees were not only made aware of the need for changes, but were given a hand in the program's implementation. The pity is that the company almost went into bankruptcy before the parties involved faced up to the true facts and took appropriate corrective action. This story is very representative and could be duplicated in many organizations.

Who can honestly blame the unions for taking advantage of a free lunch that they must neither buy nor help to cook? It's also hard to blame workers for holding the false belief that the union represents a benevolent god who can secure things for them that they'd have trouble getting by themselves. Management has permitted this state of affairs to evolve. To change this condition, management must develop a new attitude and a set of collective bargaining ground rules that both the unions and the workers accept. It must do this soon. Management has already given away most of the store while scarcely considering the cost of its inventory investment.

Here are a few suggestions designed to help management live with the union shop and still retain its right to manage.

HOW TO LIVE WITH THE UNION SHOP

Prepare for labor hearings or collective bargaining sessions as you would for a court case or an IRS audit. Management, for the most part, fails to do this. Get rid of any ideas you might have that organized labor is a semiliterate group of radicals that can be conned by a few superficial promises. Nothing could be further from the truth.

Leaders of the labor movement have been taught by experts who know all the right formulas and are not afraid to apply them. Recognize this and act accordingly. Regard the union as an equal, but only as an equal. Organized labor now has enough goodies that negotiations can be conducted on a give-and-take basis instead of on the tacit understanding that management *always* has to give something away without getting anything in return.

Conversely, never go into a labor hearing or bargaining session with a chip on your shoulder. Managers can no longer afford to feel they have the right to set all the rules simply because they happen to own the football. Management must wake up and consider the cost of the erroneous idea that it knows it all and doesn't have to be prepared to meet with labor. Each time management meets labor with a patronizing attitude, each time it treats labor negotiators as a bunch of poorly equipped schoolboys instead of the well-prepared, well-informed leaders they are, management leaves itself open to lose still another round of a contest in which, traditionally, management has come out second best.

If plans are being developed for changes like building a new plant, making a change in the management structure, buying another company, closing a plant or division for a while, or expanding a department, tell your employees about it. *And tell them first.* Management is privy to policy changes before anyone else. Isn't it a bit ridiculous to get scooped on this type of information by the labor press?

Programs involving employee participation should never be implemented without first selling the supervisory group on the change. This applies to job-evaluation plans, time-and-motion studies, merit rating, or any other programs affecting employee take-home pay or fringe benefits. Better still, assign the supervisors a role in developing these plans. We all like to be told in advance. Therefore, once you've sold a plan or policy to supervision, spend a little additional time selling it to your workers. Giving them advance information will enable them to see and appreciate the advantages instead of just the shortcomings that may be exaggerated through the rumor mill.

I feel strongly enough about this that in the course of several presentations I have made to management groups I've taken the trouble to prepare a prescription bottle containing three capsules. I distribute these items to each of the members of the audience with the explanation, "This medicine, if used properly, can cure most of your management's ills. Since I am not a physician the capsules do not, needless to say, contain any drugs or conventional healing powers. Instead, inside each of the three capsules is a small piece of paper containing a single piece of advice. The three comments are as follows:

1. Information breeds understanding.
2. We all want to be told in advance.
3. We will all cooperate in a program in the same proportion that we are part of that program."

SELLING YOUR WORKERS

American management is supposed to be the best in the world when it comes to selling its products, but it has done a miserable job of selling itself to the American worker. If your workers are forced to depend on the union, the grapevine, or rumors at the corner beer joint for their information, your present program simply isn't accomplishing its purpose. Management must do something about its problem of convincing employees that it cares about their welfare.

When was the last time you took a hard look at your employee-evaluation program? How does it operate? Is it a vital part of the administrative policy or is it simply considered a necessary evil by the people responsible for its overall function? A well-run job-evaluation program gives management much more than an insight into individual performance. It is a morale improvement factor and it can bring to light facts to talk about during labor negotiations.

Does your company have a workable policy for promotion from within? Do your workers believe in it? Has any clear-cut policy been established so that workers may improve their status within the organization? This is one area where management is usually not in competition with the union, since it is to the union's advantage *not* to lose its membership to the ranks of management.

Are wages, benefits, and other personnel policies and practices in line with the industry and the area? Have any studies been made about this? If not, why not? Is your company interested in community affairs? Is the community interested in your company? This is an important factor is you are required to draw on local labor supply. An occasional press release to your local newspaper concerning company affairs and events can do wonders for your company image.

Many managers tend to forget that the most valuable commodity in their organization is the people who make it function. It's surprising how a little idea such as letting employees select from three color schemes for a plant or office can perk up morale. A simple voting measure adds to the pride employees have in the place where they work and at the same time makes them feel a little more important.

An effective device to assure better employee communications is to check with employees regularly to determine their current feelings toward the company. Employees should be surveyed at least every three years to determine their complaints and attitudes. When trouble spots are noted as a result of the survey, they should be corrected. And once corrections have been made it is important to report back to the workers and advise them of the action taken. Between these official surveys, ways should be devised to sample employee opinions and reactions on a day-to-day basis.

In any labor–management communications program, care should be taken to avoid trying to cram free enterprise down the employees' throats. Most of them are tired of hearing about free enterprise. They just want to live in it. Tailor your communications program to report all the news, but don't overglorify the company.

Let's face it, no one is more familiar with the shortcomings of an organization than the people who work there. Any attempt to distort facts or manage the news will immediately be obvious and further detract from management's credibility.

Some years ago I had the privilege of being included in the Japanese Productivity Conference, an honor I hastily accepted in the light of the vast productivity strides that have been accomplished by our Far East trade partners. One of the most interesting findings at these sessions was the fact that Japanese workers are consistently more dedicated to their jobs than their American counterparts. It is common practice, for example, for a Japanese worker who is entitled to three weeks of vacation to turn back one week as a show of good faith toward the employers and fellow workers.

In return for this, Japanese management evidences a remarkable goodwill toward the people who produce its goods and services, contrary to the image some people hold on the subject. Barring extremely adverse conditions, a Japanese worker is assured of a job with the company for life. Pay during sick periods, including pregnancy, goes on regardless of length of illness. Monotonous and repetitive job functions are, if possible, replaced by automation, and the people displaced are transferred with appropriate training into more creative and interesting work. Unions exist but often work hand in hand with management and sit in on management meetings, where they contribute valuable input conducive to greater job satisfaction and productivity.

In light of the labor–management climate in America, any current attempt to transplant all these policies to a Detroit auto factory would be doomed to failure. Yet there is no doubt that the empathy that normally exists between labor and management in Japan is a king-sized factor in the glaring difference between the two countries in productivity and balance-of-trade figures.

Perhaps, in view of how far labor has progressed in America, it is impractical to suggest that American workers would even consider an arrangement of this type. Changes of this scope are, admittedly, difficult to bring about. However, if our industrial leaders were unilaterally to develop a program designed to convince their employees that they truly have their interests at heart, those leaders might be surprised at the reciprocal benefits they would acquire in return.

THE COMPANY NEWSLETTER—
BENEFIT OR FARCE?

One of the most effective devices for improving labor–management relations is an employee-circulated newsletter. It can reap huge benefits in employee goodwill *providing* it is developed and prepared in a manner designed to appeal to the real interests of the workers who constitute the readership. Sadly enough, however, most company publications not only fail to improve communications, but often have an adverse effect on management–employee relations.

Ask a dozen rank-and-file employees what they think of their company's newsletter and there's a good chance most of them will freely admit they seldom bother to read it. Further questioning, particularly if done by someone outside company management, will probably produce replies like "brainwash," "propaganda," or simply "uninteresting reading." In view of the almost universal indictment of what should be one of management's most effective tools, it seems appropriate that the people who publish or formulate the policy for these publications take a hard look at what they're doing wrong and decide what, if anything, can be done to correct the unfavorable image they have created.

A primary source of reader dissatisfaction is that company-issued publications have been permitted to deteriorate into one-sided instruments that publicize only the interests of the company and management's side of any given issue. Employees have been conditioned to expect some degree of responsible journalism in a country that claims to maintain freedom of the press. After being fed a steady diet of management-controlled news over a long period of time, they strike back, either by refusing to read the offered material or by attempting to discredit it.

If you doubt that management is either being overselective or just plain "copping out" in the handling of in-house material, take a look at a typical issue of a company newsletter and then compare it with a similar publication put out by the company's union. Look at the type of material offered by the union newspaper: real down-to-earth gutsy stuff like economic facts, what union members are getting—or are going to get. By contrast, the front page of a company publication may offer a profile of the second vice-president in charge of sales, whose accomplishments or family history couldn't matter less to a bench hand working in the tool room. It interests me that in over 30 years of association with top management I have yet to see a union publication in an executive office.

More often than not the wishy-washy reporting in company newspapers stems from the fact that their editors, or employees responsible for selection of material, are operating under a severe handicap. As administrative or semiadministrative employees, editors feel that they should represent management's point of view. Yet, paradoxically, they are also charged with the responsibility of communicating with labor, which comprises the top-heavy majority of the readership. The result, unless the person responsible for the newsletter's contents is either an extreme extrovert or unusually talented in the field of written communication, is usually a lopsided version of the news, heavily weighted in favor of management.

Also, the responsibility for the newspaper's contents is too often entrusted to some barely qualified member of the office staff who just happens to have the available time to muddle through the admittedly time consuming duties with a minimum degree of effectiveness. The obvious solution is, of course, to select competent personnel to handle the program and give them the license to cover topics that are meaningful to the people who make up its readership.

Another basic fault with company publications is that they tend to fall into the habit of being issued on an irregular basis. I know of one company that issues a newsletter only when it is faced with some type of labor crisis. It is then trotted out to express management's views. Since this occurs only when the going gets rough or when the labor press is snapping at corporate fetlocks, the action fools no one, and is actually so obvious that the publication is a standing joke among employees, who laughingly refer to it as "The Management Brainwash."

If a newsletter is worth publishing, it's worth publishing on a regular basis. By getting people into the habit of expecting it, you create a condition where they will find themselves looking forward to reading what it says. This is good. If employees are informed by an official source, they don't have to settle for the distorted version of the news acquired through the company grapevine.

In the preparation and editing, care should be taken not to overglorify the company. I know of a firm that operates an extremely well run nonunion shop. Employee benefits are good and compare favorably with most union shops in the same industry.

Possibly because of this, the company has thus far managed to survive attempts by the union to organize the plant. The president of this firm is an extremely capable and knowledgeable man. He has but one serious hangup—an irrational fear of his organization's becoming organized. Since this man is also the company newsletter's editor and chief contributor, each issue contains some exaggerated and completely distorted version of the merits of his firm as a place to work. It also contains several thinly veiled references to the dire consequences that will befall his workers should they make the mistake of voting in a union shop.

At the moment, a majority of the personnel still favor a nonunion operation, but the vote gets closer each time the union makes a bid. Should the union move in, its victory will, in my opinion, have been caused primarily by the completely unrealistic propaganda this man is attempting to cram down the throats of his workers, all of whom are intelligent enough to recognize the obvious intent of his distorted editorializing.

Most company newsletters fail to answer the questions that are foremost in the minds of employees. Numerous subjects make effective copy and will generate improved labor–management relations. Subjects like the condition of the business, the outlook for the future, price situations, labor situations, wage situations, shortages, competition, legislation as it affects the business, new customers, and policy changes are all meaty material that if handled honestly will be faithfully read and even enjoyed by the work force.

Additional subjects are employee benefits, tax information, new orders, quality control, statistics, and, of course, personnel news—providing it is not top heavy with management-oriented material. Pages of pictures of the company president at ribbon-cutting ceremonies become wearisome and are often construed (sometimes rightly so) as attempts by the editorial staff to butter up the top brass. Since nonsupervisory readers probably outnumber management readers by a ratio of at least ten to one, the basic slant should be toward the worker. If an article is included that applies only to management, it should not be put in top lead position. This is an *employee* newsletter. If you want to print something for management, do it separately and circulate it exclusively among managers. If the company is large enough, you may wish to consider a separate supervisor's newsletter mailed to the supervisors' homes on a confidential basis. You might be surprised at the goodwill that can be acquired by this simple communication device.

Finally, don't ignore unsavory conditions that you know about. Face up to unpleasant facts, meet them head on, and take a position. Your readers may not always agree with your stand, but they'll appreciate your forthright presentation and honest approach. The important thing is to be sincere and present the facts, basing judgments on conditions as they exist at the time the newsletter goes to press. If it turns out you're wrong, you can change your position later. Oddly enough, even a correction of a previous statement can sometimes enhance your image in the eyes of your employees.

It takes a brave person to stand squarely up to the issues and consistently tell it like it is. But if you print a newsletter, like it or not, you're in the publishing business. And telling it like it is is what publishing is all about.

THE EMPATHY IMPROVEMENT
PROGRAM

There is a desperate need, in every segment of our economy, for some type of remedial action designed to curb the hostility between labor and management. Yet, ironically enough, few comprehensive programs have been designed to accomplish this. The problem appears to stem from the fact that, unlike work measurement, safety, cost control, and a host of other management devices, communications is a difficult thing to assess in quantitative terms. Because of this, it is frequently brushed under the rug and regarded as something that might get better at some future date if we make a few superficial changes. This hardly ever happens, of course, because any real improvement involves a complete reassessment of the attitudes and values of both labor, management, and supervision.

A program that comes closest to accomplishing this is one I developed some years back when I was associated with Rockwell Manufacturing Company. It was extremely successful and was later used, with appropriate modifications, in numerous other companies with results that can only be described as spectacular. It works in both union and nonunion shops. All it takes to implement this program is to recognize that there is a problem and to convince all parties in the organization that the company is serious about better labor–management communications, followed by the will and determination to do something about this important subject.

The program begins with the distribution of two separate questionnaires, one for supervisors and the other for all employees. In both instances the questionnaires involve only yes or no answers, and management should emphasize that names are not to be signed. Management should also point out that the survey is not designed to point out *employee weaknesses*; on the contrary, it is designed to bring to light the *weaknesses of current company programs and policies*.

While the actual questions would necessarily vary from one company to another, Figure 7-1 gives examples of questions that might be asked:

Figure 7.1

QUESTIONS FOR SUPERVISORS	Yes	No
1. Do you know what steps to take to handle a grievance?	____	____
2. Do you understand the basis on which employees are promoted?	____	____
3. Do employees in your department come to you for help?	____	____
If so, do they discuss fairly freely their personal problems with you?	____	____
4. Do you relay both good and bad news to employees when it affects them?	____	____
5. Do you allow employees to use their own judgment?	____	____
6. Do you watch for effective performance that would indicate that an employee could be moved up?	____	____
7. Do you alert your superiors when you see unusually good traits in an employee?	____	____
8. Would you keep a promise even though it conflicted with company policy?	____	____
9. Do you feel you can give an employee straight facts when required to pass down unpleasant news?	____	____
10. Do you believe that management sincerely wants		

employees to be kept informed of progress, developments, and the like? ____ ____

11. Do you believe that employees have a clear understanding of management problems, such as the need for profit, the need to keep costs down, and so on? ____ ____

12. Do you discuss practices and policy changes with employees in connection with the following?

General company policies? ____ ____

Company benefits? ____ ____

Wages? ____ ____

Safety? ____ ____

13. Do you encourage employees to submit suggestions? ____ ____

Do you help them with suggestions? ____ ____

14. Would you *personally* discuss the following with one of your employees or would you leave it for someone else to do? ____ ____

An employee gets a raise? (telling how he or she earned it) ____ ____

A promotion? (telling why he or she got it) ____ ____

A transfer? (telling him or her why) ____ ____

A reprimand? (telling him or her why) ____ ____

15. Do you believe there is sufficient *written* communication for employees, such as newsletters, bulletin boards, and letters from management? ____ ____

16. Do you think there should be more *oral* communication, such as meetings and face-to-face discussion? ____ ____

17. Do you feel that the company, through its oral and written communications, is giving employees the information they want and need? ____ ____

18. Do you feel that you have problems you need help in solving but are unsure of whom to approach for help? ____ ____

After a tabulation of the results of this questionnaire (which will point out areas that need attention), a meeting of all supervisors should be held, at which time a report should be made on the survey findings. Subjects that according to the survey need clarification should be listed and supervisors asked to indicate their importance in 1, 2, 3 order.

Following this, an announcement should be made of a new type of supervisory program to be established on company time. Subjects to be covered should be taken from the supervisors' own lists and presented in the order of importance as they rated them.

What might typical topics be? In one company, where a method similar to this was used, supervisors chose the following in order of importance and need:

1. State of the business (how are we doing?)
2. Future company plans (business outlook?)
3. Supervisor status (job clarification)
4. Company policy (supervisors admitted they needed guidance in day-to-day human relations with their own people)

The meetings will produce more if they are kept small (15 to 20 people). Following discussion of the problems, solutions should be presented, and when supervisors feel they have the proper formula, it is presented to management for approval as policy. If approved, these policy decisions will be written up and put in a binder issued to each supervisor, and, finally, will become part of the official revised policy manual.

Simultaneously with the survey relative to supervisory personnel, another questionnaire should be submitted to all employees in the organization. Again, employees should be urged to answer sincerely and honestly and cautioned that no names are to be signed. A list of typical questions that might be contained in the questionnaire appears in Figure 7.2.

Figure 7.2

QUESTIONS FOR EMPLOYEES	Yes	No
1. Are you proud to tell people you work for Acme Company?	___	___
2. If you were starting all over again, would you go to work for Acme Company?	___	___
3. Do you consider Acme a friendly place to work?	___	___

4. Do you feel that Acme Company keeps you informed of company affairs that affect you or might affect you? _____ _____

5. Do you know practically all the company's products? _____ _____

6. Do you know who our chief competitors are? _____ _____

7. Would you like a regular report on our products and their uses? _____ _____

8. Would you like a regular report on how the company is doing? _____ _____

9. Where do you get *most* of your *company* information? _____ _____

   Bulletin boards? _____ _____

   Newsletter? _____ _____

   Management directives? _____ _____

   Supervisor? _____ _____

   Meetings? _____ _____

   Grapevine? _____ _____

10. Do you know whom you should see if you have any questions concerning the following? _____ _____

    Personnel policies? _____ _____

    Wage rates? _____ _____

    Rules and regulations? _____ _____

    Your gripes? _____ _____

    Suggestions and ideas? _____ _____

11. Would you feel free to go to these people to discuss these matters? _____ _____

12. If you ask a question about any of the matters mentioned above, do you usually get a satisfactory answer? _____ _____

13. Do you understand what's expected of you on your job? _____ _____

14. Does your supervisor discuss your job with you and tell you how you're doing? _____ _____

15. Would you like to have a regular appraisal and review of your performance given to you by your supervisor? _____ _____

16. Do you feel credit is given you when you've earned it? _____ _____

17. Are you satisfied with your job? _____ _____

18. Are your working conditions satisfactory? _____ _____

19. Do you feel you received sufficient training for   ____ ____
your job?

20. Do you feel that promotion policy at Acme Com-   ____ ____
pany is fair and that your qualifications for promotion would be given full consideration?

21. About your own supervisor (no names, please):

Is he or she fair?   ____ ____

Does he or she give credit when it's due?   ____ ____

Does your supervisor keep promises?   ____ ____

Are you advised promptly of changes or develop-   ____ ____
ments that might affect you?

Do you feel that your supervisor fulfills his or her   ____ ____
responsibilities?

You may make any comment you wish on the other side of this sheet.
We *do not* want you to sign your name, but it would help us to get a
better idea of employee opinion if you would tell us if you are:

Male employee____

Female employee____

Shop employee____   Office employee____

Supervisor____

Years of service with the company____years

DO NOT SIGN YOUR NAME

Following receipt of the completed questionnaires, management should tabulate the results as quickly as possible and provide
each employee with a printout of the results. At the same time the
company should announce plans to correct "trouble areas."

Corrective action should include a request for all members of
top and middle management to analyze the survey findings and
provide a list of specific actions that will be taken with respect to the
problem or problems. These should be submitted to an area manager, who in turn should prepare a report to all employees in the division. The report will outline the findings and the corrective measures planned.

In six months, each location, division, and area manager
should report to his or her superior exactly what has been done to
follow up on the proposed actions. From these reports and subse-

quent follow-up reports, a progress report should be prepared giving examples of what has been accomplished. The progress reports should be mailed to each employee in the organization.

The results of this type of audit normally are favorable beyond all expectations. Employees feel that their viewpoints have not only been listened to but also acted on. Mid-level management people similarly report a vast improvement in attitude and morale.

The degree of success will normally depend on the degree of involvement and follow-up provided by top management. And it is here that management must act as the catalyst in bringing the program to a successful climax. Top management simply cannot afford to be "too busy" to provide vigorous support.

In fact, having asked both workers and supervisors to participate in the survey, part of the program should also include a questionnaire in which top management takes a long, hard look at its own policies and attitudes. I call this portion of the program the "Management Self-Audit." Typical questions here might include:

1. Are top management members sincerely interested in our employees, their needs, and their problems? Or is top management interested solely in the profit picture?

2. Do members of top management make any effort to keep in touch with rank-and-file thinking? One company's board chairman personally visited the work areas and shook hands with *every* employee when he took over his duties. The president of another company maintains a file of all employees. Each week he pulls a card at random, and the employee whose name is drawn is asked to come to the president's office for a visit. The employee is put at ease and numerous subjects are discussed, in which the employee is asked for his or her frank opinion. Employees anticipate and enjoy these visits.

3. Do our employees know members of top management? By name, or simply by sight? One company president makes it a point several times each month to enter the plant by the "back door" and walk through the shop, chatting with employees as he moves along.

4. Have we made any effort to tell employees about management problems?

5. Have we ever asked for employees' cooperation in helping to solve some of our problems? One company placed a banner headline on its employee publication titled: "WE LOST MONEY LAST YEAR . . . We need your help . . . Here's what you can do to help

us get back in the black." Details followed and subsequent regular reports were made to employees, crediting them with cooperation and for helping to turn the tide.

6. Have we initiated a practical, workable method by which our employees can get their views to top management? In short, how effective is our *two-way* communication? Some companies survey employees regularly to get expressions of opinion. Others conduct "inquiring photographer" columns in their magazines and newspapers. Some firms use "Idea Derby" contests as adjuncts to the suggestion system. From time to time certain companies will send out self-addressed, postage-paid cards inviting questions.

7. Do our employees feel they belong? What are we doing to make them feel a part of the company? In some companies, when the purchase of new equipment is contemplated, management invites recommendations concerning make, model, and so on. Highly favorable results have been reported from this policy. Employees take much better care of equipment they have helped to select and strive for peak production from it. Other organizations underwrite the cost of the supervisor taking people in his or her department out to dinner occasionally to meet with them informally and go over facts and figures at the same time. Often these social conferences are linked to the annual report.

8. Does our company have a satisfactory grievance setup? Do employees know the various individuals and steps to be taken if the supervisor's decision is unsatisfactory? Do we really study the grievances in order to keep ourselves informed of possible "trouble areas?"

This is by no means a complete self-audit for management. Many additional questions could be asked, but these may help lay the groundwork for an appraisal of ourselves.

The success of the program will depend on vigorous follow-through and active participation by all parties concerned. It must be an ongoing project that cannot be permitted to lapse into something that is only accorded lip service after a short period of time.

Some guidelines to ensure a viable communications program follow.

GUIDELINES FOR TOP MANAGEMENT

1. *Be sincere. You can't make red out of blue.* Modern communication between employer and employee has, in a dangerous number of instances, consisted of pure propaganda for the employer. In these in-

stances the communicators have overlooked the fact that their job is to build goodwill and understanding. Instead they try to spread a favorable smokescreen around the organization. Communication must be honest and sincere to be successful. Otherwise, it may enjoy acceptance for a time, but inevitably employees will look with mistrust on management statements.

2. *Be simple and unaffected in your language.* Whether it's oral or printed communication, be conversational. Many management messages are stuffy and uninteresting. Talking to employees involves a conversation, not a commencement address.

3. *Don't overglorify the company.* Harsh as it may sound to the sentimentalists, the plant is a place of brick and mortar and glass. It's full of people with good habits and bad habits, with pleasing dispositions and disagreeable personalities. If it's a normal organization, it has had triumphs, disappointments, labor serenity, and labor strife. To attempt to paint it as an industrial Eden is an insult to your worker's intelligence.

4. *Select competent personnel to handle the communications program.* A successful communications program requires people of many practical talents, including meeting employees and getting along with them, writing simply and sensibly, knowing what constitutes a story and how to put it together, and great tact combined with sincerity of purpose.

5. *Make communications a top-level management responsibility.* If a communications program is to be effective, it must have the blessing, encouragement, and cooperation of the front office. The industrial editor or communications director working ten notches down on the industrial totem pole, with no access to the policy-making level, is as ineffective as a wax spark plug. If the program is to reflect top management thinking, the person who is to interpret that thinking must be directly exposed to it. Chief executives simply cannot afford to evade the issue with the weak argument that they're too busy to give personal attention to anything as vital as the people who produce their goods or services.

6. *Don't ignore unsavory situations your employees know to exist.* If your program is to have acceptance, be realistic. If you have labor trouble, talk about it. If the plant has been struck, say so. If you have unpleasant situations that your own people are discussing, have the courage to discuss them sincerely and openly. Employees hear enough double-talk from our nation's politicians without being subjected to it on the job.

7. *Investigate all devices of communication and use them.* There are

numerous communication devices. Some are made to order for the large company. Others work more effectively in a small operation. The individual or group meeting with employees, involving personal contact, is the best of all. And the best single channel of communications is through the first-line supervisor.

8. *Check constantly on the effectiveness of your program.* The investment you make in a communications program should show results. They may be less tangible than the results of an advertising drive, but they can be measured. Surveys of employee opinion have become more sensible and scientific. Employees, if properly approached, will appraise communications devices frankly and sincerely.

9. *Never let your communications program slow down.* The good program is a continuing device. It's a day-in, day-out effort to provide a continuing stream of information to employees and to encourage a flow of employee reaction and opinion in return.

10. *Finally, meet the people.* There are no swamis in industry good enough to read the minds of people they don't know. Any communications experts who think they can mastermind a continuous program from behind a desk are kidding themselves. Communications, by definition, must be at least a two-way street. (See Figure 7.3)

GUIDELINES FOR DEALING
WITH SUPERVISORS

1. *Respect the chain of command.* Don't bypass supervisors in your communications. This will simply reinforce their opinion that they are little more than glorified record keepers.

2. *Build a policy manual.* Either prepare a new manual, or update the old one, by encouraging supervisors to assemble such a manual at their meetings. Supervisors need to be made part of the manual-writing process by providing input relative to their own area of authority.

3. *Underscore the supervisor's role as a member of management.* Supervisors must be convinced, and stay convinced, that they are members of management.

4. *Don't depend on the supervisory meeting as your only communications device.* Regardless of the size of the organization, the oral

Figure 7.3 Business growth increases complexity of communications

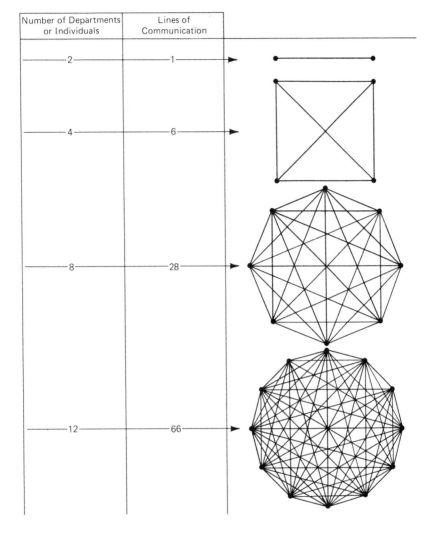

Number of Departments or Individuals	Lines of Communication
2	1
4	6
8	28
12	66

message needs written backing. Get the message across. Even if it's only in the form of a half-page letter.

5. *Prepare well for supervisory meetings.* Strive to have them efficiently run, orderly, and profitable from a supervisor's viewpoint. If the meeting is simply regarded as a necessary evil, supervisors will soon become aware of it and morale will suffer accordingly.

6. *Encourage two-way communication.* Actively seek out the opinions and attitudes of supervisors. Top management members

are usually eloquent talkers. But it's also important, at times, to be a good listener.

7. *Check your own effectiveness.* Conduct periodic self-audits together with oral and written examinations to make sure you're getting through.

8. *Review the grievance file.* Find out what's bothering the people. Study complaints to find out if there's a pattern to the criticism. Analyze them to determine if the complaints are justified.

9. *Develop a supervisory inventory in the manner outlined in Chapter Four.* Find out the strengths and weaknesses of the people who are in charge of your day-to-day operations.

10. *Make sure your supervisors are properly trained for the job they are asked to perform.* A training program similar to the one suggested in Chapter Four can do wonders for improving the effectiveness of first-line management.

GUIDELINES FOR DEALING
WITH EMPLOYEES

1. *Keep employees apprised of advancement-from-within policy.* Publicize promotions in the employee newsletter and by other means.

2. *Give individual recognition whenever possible.* Credit employees with jobs well done. Show the employee through action that he or she is more than a number on a time card.

3. *Check working conditions regularly.* Many employees rate good working conditions ahead of wages. Publicize good safety records and new equipment designed to make work easier or safer.

4. *Check with employees periodically to determine their current attitudes toward the company.* Conduct surveys and then correct trouble spots. Report actions taken back to employees. Between official surveys, keep your finger close to the pulse of employee opinions and reactions.

5. *Keep wages, benefits, and other personnel policies and practices in line with the industry and the area.* Keep employees informed of what's being done to keep the company in line with new industry improvements and innovations.

6. *Encourage employee participation.* Contests, quizzes, suggestion systems and brainstorming sessions are all excellent devices to ensure employee feedback.

7. *Emphasize job importance by showing employees the relation between and dependence of one job to another.* Employees need to know that they are part of a larger picture than the area around their own work unit.

8. *Get to know your employees better.* Walk through the plant from time to time and single out individual employees for their thinking on various subjects. Given today's average education level, many employees have something important to say. Give them a chance to do this. It will make both of you feel better.

9. *Keep employees informed.* If changes are contemplated, don't make them find out about it in the newspaper or at the corner beer joint. Tell them—and tell them first. The company cannot be credited with sincere intent if no one knows what it is doing.

10. *Ask, don't order.* Get employees to feel they are working *with* you, not for you. Today's workers will not give loyalty to a dominant executive, particularly those workers you are anxious to retain.

If pursued with tenacity and adapted as a continuing project, the program outlined above comes as near to closing the empathy gap between labor and management as anything I have ever experienced. The key word is *sincerity*.

If management is really sincere about improving communications, its voice will be heard. And as employees become aware that the program consists of more than management platitudes and front-office lip service, their attitude will often improve far beyond the most optimistic estimates.

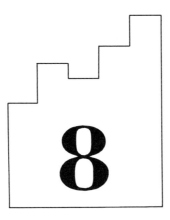

Probing Productivity Problems in Other Areas

Take away our factories, take away our trade,
our avenues of transportation, our money.
Leave us nothing but our organization, and in
four years we shall have reestablished
ourselves.

Andrew Carnegie

Given today's business climate, one might wonder if Mr. Carnegie, faced with our current problems, could have been this optimistic. There appear to be forces at work during these closing years of the twentieth century that seem intent on stifling all efforts to improve productivity. What is even more frightening is that all the efforts of our advanced technology seem unable to cope with the situation.

Why did an acceptable rate of productivity improvement exist in an earlier era and then disappear when our achievements have literally exploded into space? This question has so many facets that it is doubtful if anyone will ever come up with an explanation that is satisfactory to all concerned.

The fact remains that the situation does exist. I happen to believe that it has been caused largely by the factors described so far in this book, but additional segments in modern industry are also ailing and in great need of some vigorous therapy. Some of them are cited in this chapter, together with suggestions for improvements.

LOW WAGES DO NOT MEAN LOW COSTS

Today's bankruptcy courts are literally crammed with firms that have doggedly adhered to the erroneous principle of cheap labor. This is not to imply that the woes of American business can automatically be eliminated by the simple expedient of giving all employees a 20 percent raise. The secret lies in the not-too-unreasonable permise that management has a right to expect a fair day's work for a fair day's pay.

Indisputable surveys have consistently indicated that strict adherence to minimum wage scales invariably results in less than minimum performance. Conversely, employees who are carefully selected and given work conditions that are conducive to pride of accomplishment in their work will, on a dollar-for-dollar basis, improve their productivity far in excess of the additional wages expended.

Most businesspeople thought Henry Ford was a madman when he announced, in 1914, that he was raising the minimum wage for plant workers from $2.34 to a hitherto unheard of $5 a day. It simply wouldn't work, they said. Labor cost would eat up all the profits. The employees would simply take the extra money and stay drunk. Yet Ford Motor Company has lasted longer than most of its detractors.

Later Ford would say, "The payment of $5 for an eight-hour day was one of the finest cost-cutting moves we ever made, and the $6 day was cheaper than the $5 day."

Unfortunately, Ford's insight into labor costs still eludes many management people today. All too many U.S. companies, including Ford, have purchased labor peace by giving workers more than their productivity justifies. An example of this is the steel industry where, according to statistics from the American Iron and Steel Institute, wages and benefits for a ten year period ending in 1981 rose 221 percent while productivity rose 15.2 percent. Operating on this type of industrial arithmetic, is it any wonder that the steel industry is in trouble?

On the contrary, time after time companies have been able to boost profits by raising wages *providing* the pay increases were accompanied by increased performance, improved work methods, and formal measures of accountability.

An example of this involves a program at Muskegon Piston Ring Company, the largest manufacturer of piston rings in the world. In 1975 the automotive original-equipment division at the Muskegon plant was losing $1 million a year and operating at 40 percent of capacity. With the cooperation of the union, the company decided to raise both the base pay and production requirements for employees. Due to this, the company reversed its financial position from a $1 million annual loss to a $1 million annual profit. Plant equipment during this period was operating at 80 percent and take-home pay rose by 70 cents an hour.

Or consider Eclipse Incorporated, a Rockford, Illinois, manufacturer of industrial heating equipment, with some 650 employees. In 1978 employee turnover was 95 percent per year. Daily absenteeism ran about 10 percent and there had been a five-year slide in earnings.

The company decided to offer wage incentives based on individual and overall company performance and merit reviews of all employees, including supervisors, on a regular schedule. Wages rose by 34 percent over three years. Employee turnover was reduced to 20 percent per year and absenteeism to less than 3 percent. Meanwhile, shipping volume per employee rose 65 percent and company profits jumped 600 percent.

Each of these instances required cooperation with employees or the labor union. In each instance the problems could be traced to a sharp drop in productivity that was neither recognized nor acknowledged by employees or the union. Once the facts were made irrefutably clear, labor cooperated, particularly when it realized the changes could be beneficial to labor as well as management.

For companies the advantages were clear. With good wages accompanied by controls and standards of accountability, a company is in a position to:

- Attract better employees, pay them better than average wages, and expect more from them.
- Motivate people to produce because they want to produce.
- Insist on high productivity and refuse to tolerate anything but good overall quality and performance.

Put another way, for average wages a company will normally obtain average productivity. For high wages a company might expect to get high productivity. But it doesn't. It gets *exceptionally* high productivity.

TAMING THE PAPER TIGER

So much has been written about the need to improve paper work procedures that the paper used to publish all this information may well exceed the paper savings derived from publication of this material. Nonetheless, a few decades ago the paper-work requirements for a small company could be neatly (or not so neatly) contained in the pigeonholes of a roll-top desk. Today the same operation will probably require several file cabinets and a couple of full-time office clerks. Larger operators have been forced to add anywhere from five to fifty additional employees simply to cope with assorted forms, invoices, carbon copies, and other miscellaneous scraps of paper.

This paper-work explosion has been brought about by a variety of reasons. Cost control and analysis have, to a large degree, replaced country bookkeeping. Data processing has a voracious appetite for fresh paper. Xerox machines are often overworked simply because they exist. Government regulations gobble up a vast array of forms and reports.

Can this paper-work monster be eliminated? Probably not. Contrary to much publicity by AT&T to persuade the public to conduct business by telephone (much of which is in the form of the printed word), paper-work, if properly used, is a valuable administrative tool. It provides written evidence, it establishes responsibility for issuing an order, it eliminates duplication of instructions, and it generates goodwill.

Nevertheless, *excessive* paper-work is a factor that cuts deeply into the operating costs of a majority of today's organizations. Fortunately, there are ways by which this paper tiger can be controlled, even if it cannot be eliminated entirely.

The most effective method for doing this is a sweeping and comprehensive program designed to challenge the need for each type of communication currently being used. The program should start with the company's file cabinets. Every file cabinet in the office, when full, represents several thousand dollars' worth of clerical effort. Add to this the initial cost of equipment, floor space that could be used to better advantage, and time wasted by people who have to review copies of forms and memoranda that serve little practical purpose and the staggering cost of this paper-work begins to come sharply into focus.

In challenging the need for the items contained in file cabinets, it is well to be guided by a few basic questions. (1) How important is the information, really? (2) Is it duplicated elsewhere? (3) What would happen if we didn't have it? Answer these question honestly and very often you'll find that file storage areas can literally be cut in half.

Another costly practice is the age-old system of supplying each branch or section with a copy of everything that might remotely concern its operation. This is a throwback to the old army system, where military protocol demanded that every portion in the chain of command be advised of the movements of each unit. It has no place in modern business and should be eliminated except where the need for it is completely obvious.

The use (rather, abuse) of unnecessary forms is another area where huge savings can be accomplished. Too often we find that forms are poorly prepared, serve little useful purpose, or because of changed conditions contain information that is ineffective or could be secured elsewhere. Unnecessary forms can often be eliminated by an analysis of all the forms used by an organization, asking the following questions: (1)Is the information needed? (2)Is another source available? (3)Does the cost of obtaining the information exceed its worth? In conducting this analysis you will often find that two or three forms can be combined in a manner that actually increases their efficiency because it helps to tell the complete story.

Still another area for improvement in paper-work procedures is the interoffice memo. Savings of a significant nature can be acquired by streamlining procedures used for interoffice communications. This can be done simply by conducting a survey based on these questions and followed by appropriate action.

1. Does everyone to whom this correspondence is directed understand it?
2. Can the number of people to whom correspondence is routed be reduced?
3. Can check boxes be used to reduce the amount of routing information?
4. Can office symbols be used for routing?
5. Will the use of colored paper help in the distribution of these items?
6. Are all memos of a standard size for convenient filing?
7. Is the memo's subject clearly stated in the upper-right corner for quick location in the files?
8. Can a window envelope be used?
9. Can self-mailers be used?

DESIGNING A BETTER SUGGESTIONS PROGRAM

Whether it consists of a wooden box next to the time clock that is emptied periodically or a full-scale program requiring the services of several employees, a suggestions program can be a valuable device that, if properly designed and monitored, will result in important cost savings with an added incentive bonus to workers who are close enough to an operation to observe areas where improvement might be indicated. Unfortunately, the suggestions system as it is employed today is often expensive to operate and frequently results in a lowering of morale on the part of employees who must, of necessity, face rejection of ideas that were submitted in good faith.

The greatest single threat to any suggestions program is the lack of a positive attitude on the part of the people who analyze and evaluate the suggestions. If a suggestions system is to work, management must refrain from taking the all-too-familar attitude that if an idea were any good someone would have already thought of it. Admittedly, not all suggestions can be implemented. A report compiled by the National Association of Suggestion Systems states that only 25 percent of the suggestions offered in a given year are subsequently accepted. In most cases the rejection is warranted. Often disapproval is based on factors that were unknown to the suggester. In many instances the cost of implementation would exceed the benefits derived. Nevertheless, in numerous instances valuable suggestions are summarily dismissed because of snap judgments and arbitrary decisions.

The importance of getting several evaluations prior to passing judgment on a suggestion cannot be emphasized too strongly. The most effective way to do this, and one that is *not* employed by the majority of today's organizations, is the chain-of-command approach in which the initial evaluation is performed by the employee's immediate supervisor, after which the file is passed up the administrative ladder until it reaches someone with authority either to implement or to conclusively reject the proposal. Under this method, suggestions approved and implemented at a low management level are subsequently forwarded directly to the Suggestion Awards Committee, thus significantly diminishing the not inconsiderable amount of paper shuffling that usually accompanies a program of this type.

It could be argued that under this method top management runs the risk of losing control. However, the huge paper-work savings, combined with the additional and badly needed prestige for lower-level managers, will more than offset the risk of an occasional bad decision. Furthermore, the problem can be partially overcome by placing a member of top management on the Suggestion Awards Committee or by having work orders pertaining to suggestions channeled through a member of top management.

An extremely sensitive area in any suggestions program is what to do about proposals that must be rejected. This often requires considerable tact—especially in borderline cases where some benefits are obvious but the cost of placing the idea into effect would be prohibitive. A verbal rejection, unless the person chosen for this detail is extremely skilled in employee relations, may often do more harm than good and can frequently deteriorate into a bitter dispute. To take the sting out of rejection, a personal letter (*not a form letter!*) will usually result in a minimum of resentment, particularly if the door is left open for some recourse in the event that a mistake has been made or that events cause a change in thinking on the subject.

Another area where controversy occurs is in the amount of money to be awarded for adopted suggestions. Many businesses award 10 percent of the first year's savings to the suggester. However, suggestions concerning issues like safety and training involve intangible benefits, so some additional yardstick must be devised. A minimum award of say, $20 with an upward scale for unusually beneficial proposals would appear to be reasonable in instances of this type.

Like all other facets of modern business, a suggestions program must contain two basic ingredients. The first is a reasonable return to the company for the money it invests for implementation. The second is fair compensation to the people who contribute their time and effort to making the enterprise work.

SELLING PRODUCTIVITY TO THE
SALES DIVISION

Programs designed to cut costs, develop better standards, increase work output, or reduce inefficiency have become a standard practice in American business. Methods employed to accomplish these measures include stopwatch techniques, complex charts, expensive consultants, and even computer analysis that can be programmed to almost every area of a company's operation.

Nearly all these plans are directed primarily against operations, which includes direct and sometimes indirect labor. This is ironic because operations is an area that even in normal times is under continual scrutiny from supervision at all levels. Almost always overlooked is the fact that the sales division, which is the direct key to higher earnings, has more often than not been permitted to operate with a minimum degree of guidance and with few attempts to initiate any system of checks and balances.

The premise that a sales division can best operate under a hands-off policy is often rationalized by the argument that the salesperson is closer to the customers than anyone else and is therefore better able to determine their needs and degree of receptiveness to a company's products. Another argument for a hands-off policy is that a salesperson's income is contingent upon sales, and therefore salespeople will take it upon themselves to do whatever is necessary to move a maximum amount of the company's products.

With all due respect to the American salespeople—most of whom are competent, knowledgeable, and receptive to fresh ideas—the premise that salespeople operate best without any guidelines or restraint is as invalid as the flat-earth theory! Salespeople, while admittedly interested in making sales, are also human and therefore in need of (and often desperately desirous of) some comprehensive guidelines, or at the very least an overall operating policy that is geared to sales. Considerable evidence shows that top management in many industries has failed to provide this necessary ingredient.

Management in these companies is going to have to face up to the indisputable fact that the sales force is an important facet of the operation. It can literally make or break an organization. Therefore it should at the very least be subject to the same rules of management operation and control as the people who operate a lathe or an office typewriter.

Granted, the art of selling requires considerable sublety and tact and is not the sort of thing that can normally be resolved by a canned list of do's and don'ts. Nevertheless, observations made at a number of different companies have turned up a surprising number of recurring weaknesses, either in the sales operation or in the manner by which top management is directing that operation. Here are some illustrations of these areas of difficulty, together with suggested remedial action.

1. *Salespeople are often allowed to sell what they want rather than what the company directs them to sell.* This is basically a management problem and stems from lack of communication between the sales force and top management. Frequently, salespeople are treated as subordinates by top management and sales managers. Seldom are they advised on a company's internal problems or the profit structure on various products. Consequently, they often go into the field with only a vague knowledge of exactly what is expected of them.

The problem will probably not be resolved by half-measures or by the company president delivering a superficial pep talk at the next sales meeting. What is needed is a better sales staff—management relationship, followed by a comprehensive training program for salespeople in which it is clearly outlined exactly what the company wishes to accomplish, what it hopes to sell, and what its priorities, its capabilities, and its shortcomings are. This action should then be backed up by a complete reevaluation of sales incentives based on a graduated scale of percentages that are proportionate to the lines that management most hopes to sell.

2. *Salespeople often concentrate on the big order and give only perfunctory attention to other propects that, with a little attention, could develop into a sizeable source of additional revenue.* In some cases this policy has even been endorsed by managers who either issue instructions not to take on small accounts or, as happens more frequently, give tacit approval when salepeople turn up their noses at small orders.

There is probably no greater practical illustration of the futility of putting all one's eggs in the same basket than a competitive operation like selling. Despite this, many salespeople, and in some cases their employers, appear content to sit smugly on a few large accounts, complacent in the knowledge that repeat orders will continue to roll in with the same regularity as the monthly telephone bill.

One of the most distressing facts of life for the business person is that a continual influx of *new* business is necessary to offset the attrition of gross revenue caused by lost accounts. This is an elementary law of business survival.

3. *Most companies fail to reapportion sales efforts in a manner designed to motivate the sales staff on a basis of equipment utilization.* It is an unusual company that does not possess at least one piece of equipment that is idle to a degree where it fails to justify the floor space it occupies and the maintenance required to keep it in working order. Yet, oddly enough, seldom is any meaningful effort made to secure enough additional work to keep this equipment in operation. Again, this is not the fault of the sales division. It is a top management problem. The solution lies in providing the salespeople with a sound working knowledge of the organization that pays their salaries and then developing incentives for sales personnel designed to make greater use of equipment that might otherwise be idle.

4. *Many salespeople lack a comprehensive knowledge of the entire industry as opposed to the product they are trying to sell.* With a better background in the needs of the industry and the manner in which it operates, salespeople are in a better position to anticipate the needs of the customers as well as talk to them about their own problems

and how to resolve them. One means of creating this ideal situation is, of course, to hire salespeople who have a background in the industry in which they are trying to sell. Since this is not always possible or practical, the best alternative is to include in the sales training curriculum at least some general information about the industry.

Too many management people lose sight of the fact that the people with whom a salesperson must associate are quite knowledgeable about the industry that provides them with their bread and butter. These people might be much more receptive to doing business with someone who has at least taken the trouble to learn the difference between a parapet and a parakeet.

5. *Too many salespeople are paid on gross sales rather than on percentage of profit to the company.* It is one of the basic laws of economics that everyone loves a bargain. Accordingly, the customer who is looking for a bargain can be expected to direct more attention to items on which the company makes a relatively small margin of profit. The problem is further complicated by the fact that a salesperson who is paid on gross sales can be expected to push the items that are easiest to sell.

The solution is a commission structure based on percentage of profit to the company. There's no denying that this involves some work, presents some problems, and requires more bookkeeping than a policy based on gross sales. Nevertheless, the modified procedure can pay huge dividends for a company and is usually welcomed by the more competent sales personnel for the obvious reason that they can make more money.

6. *Sales managers often lack the qualifications to provide meaningful leadership to the sales force they are supposed to direct.* In many instances sales managers appear content to function in a figurehead status, with little or no thought of developing guidelines or providing operating policy for the department they are supposed to oversee. Another frequent complaint is that many sales managers forget the necessity of getting into the field often enough to know problems firsthand. Because of this, they may develop a distorted viewpoint, based on second- or third-hand information. Many of today's sales managers achieved their present status because they originally were top salespeople. This is fine if they possess the qualities of leadership necessary for the job. However, the criteria for a good sales manager and a good salesperson have no more similarity than the criteria for a high production worker and a good supervisor. In ei-

ther case, if the company promotes a person solely on the basis of performance on the old job, it may find that it has lost a good producer and gained a poor supervisor.

7. *Salespeople, because of the competitive nature of their occupation, tend to work primarily for themselves rather than for the company*. This characteristic extends, at times, to withholding information and techniques that would be helpful to other salespeople working for the same company. The practice is particularly prevalent when a firm generates sales competition through the use of contests and other gimmicks designed to pit one salesperson against another.

A degree of information sharing can often be achieved by requesting each saleperson to make a brief presentation before the entire sales group and in the presence of top management. At this meeting each salesperson is asked to describe what type of sales technique has been particularly successful in his or her case.

The knowledge that they are presenting this information to top management, as well as to their peers, will, more often than not, motivate salespeople to come up with their *best* pitch—if for no other reason than to make a better presentation to top management.

8. *Many salespeople are burdened with excess paper work*. During periods of economic crisis, most companies cut overhead in the front office, and in the process they often load the resultant paper work on the sales force.

When we consider the comparative value to the company of a first-rate office clerk and a first-rate salesperson, it becomes clear that if a salesperson is losing effective selling time by performing credit checks or some similar type of office chore, he or she is not operating at maximum effectiveness. Add to this the fact that many salespeople are not really qualified for this type of work and it becomes painfully obvious that the company is indirectly paying a price all out of proportion to what the job is really worth.

Generally, salespeople should be required to do only two things as far as paper work is concerned: call reports and expense reports.

9. *Salespeople make too many promises that can't be kept*. This problem is extremely prevalent and falls squarely on the shoulders of the sales division manager. Unlike the sale of sand from a bottomless pit, the sale of most manufactured products is contingent on availability of equipment and skilled personnel. In spite of this, many salespeople promise services that cannot be provided and set deadlines that cannot be kept. True, some jobs are complex and might

conceivably be difficult to estimate. Nevertheless, when a company fails for the third or fourth time to provide services contracted in good faith, the customer can be expected to react with something short of complete impassiveness.

The solution to this problem is so obvious that it is one of the mysteries of life why the problem occurs so often. Salespeople who have not learned enough about the physical layout of a plant to make an intelligent estimate should contact someone in operations before setting dates, rather than making any promises that are based on sheer guesswork.

10. *Management often fails to keep the sales force informed.* This is another of the many problems that must be shared jointly between top management and the sales division. Good salespeople often make a conscious effort to keep up with changes that occur within the industry in general and their own company in particular. Yet all too often management, by failing to recognize the sales force as an important part of the operation, invites situations in which salespeople are unaware of factors that are obvious to everyone else from the company president to the night watchman.

The solution, of course, lies in improved communications concerning things like business outlook for the future, price situations, policy changes, new customers, new competition, and a variety of other topics that should be called to the attention of the sales force on a regular basis.

Salespeople, because of their conversational abilities, often give the impression of being extroverts. Nevertheless, they have feelings, too, and morale problems. By keeping them informed you'll convince them you have their interest at heart and perhaps improve the total operation in the process.

The items noted here are all *recurring* problems and comprise only the most obvious areas of difficulty that exist between management and the sales force that sells its product. From these observations, and stated in the most charitable manner possible, it must be concluded that a huge empathy gap presently exists between the people who produce the product and those who sell the merchandise. In most of the cases noted, the solutions are better communications between operations and sales and a sales division that is exposed to the same management rules as the rest of the corporate structure.

As the pressures of the economy increase, we will probably be forced into some of the remedies pointed out in the previous pages.

It is high time we recognized the sales division as neither an untouchable nor one of industry's stepchildren, but rather as an important function of the business structure that is subject to the same rules observed by co-workers in operations.

THE CASE FOR QUALITY CONTROL

"The appalling lack of quality control in America is a serious contributing factor to our declining rate of productivity." When I made this statement to a business associate recently, he countered with the statement, "It might be a factor, yet in the strict sense of the word, quality control tends to somewhat inhibit productivity by taking workers who might be productively employed and reassigning them to nonproductive duties and additional paper shuffling." This attitude is, unfortunately, shared by many of today's industrialists.

It may brand me as something of a maverick, but I must strongly disagree with the premise that quality control does not pay for its own personnel expenditures! Those of us who grew up in the 1930s can vividly recall the Japanese products that filled the counters of our nation's department stores. They consisted of watches that didn't work, wind-up toys that ceased to function the day after Christmas, and papier-mâché knicknacks that were given away at the local movie houses on bingo nights. The commodities imported from Japan in those days were cheaper than their American counterparts, yet the law-mandated inscription "Made in Japan" was all that was required to generate a huge "buy American" movement despite the worst economic depression in our history. The notion of Japanese inferiority in the field of manufacturing was slow to die, even after Japan began racking up huge productivity gains while American factories were struggling to barely balance productivity improvement with increased operating costs.

"Sure they're producing more," was the consumer attitude, "but look at the quality of the merchandise. American products are constructed better. So they're worth a little more." You don't hear much of this kind of talk any more, except perhaps on some of the TV automobile commercials.

American industry must face up to the unpleasant fact that Japanese vehicles are a far cry from the worthless junk that was synonymous with Japanese products of another era. They are, for the most part, well built, gas efficient, and constructed under standards of quality control that are virtually unheard of on American assembly lines.

The auto industry is, of course, only one segment of the industrial scene where Japan and other countries have made deep inroads into America's share of the market. Makers of TV sets, musical instruments, motorcycles, and other products too numerous to mention no longer hide the "Made in Japan" label on an inconspicuous area of their products, but openly and proudly advertise the origin of manufacture in full-page magazine displays and spot TV commercials. When they can be persuaded to emerge from behind their corporation's public-relations smoke screen, many American industrialists reluctantly agree that American-made products are generally more prone to defects than their overseas counterparts. When approached about building factories in the United States to take some of our unemployed auto workers off the unemployment rolls, Japanese car makers bluntly state they are afraid to build factories in America because they fear the quality of our labor.

The apathy of American industrialists toward strong quality control measures seems to be based on the premise that quality control can be lumped together with operations like safety, environmental impact regulations, and other government-controlled indirect labor factors that must be absorbed as part of the cost of doing business. And since quality control is the least-regulated factor it is also the first to fall under the ax of cost-cutting measures.

This is short-sighted reasoning. A vigorous program of quality control will return benefits far in excess of the work-hours required to implement the procedure. Quality control, or lack of it, affects productivity in the following ways.

1. Complaints about product defects must be processed. This requires additional administrative work-hours and time spent in complaint investigation.
2. Defective products still under warranty must be replaced at company expense.
3. Minor problems that could be corrected as they occur become major problems if left unchecked.
4. Customer dissatisfaction results in fewer sales and a lower share of the market.

Since there seems little room for doubt that we have been out-maneuvered in both quality control and productivity by foreign countries, particularly Japan, it seems appropriate that we consider not only what *we* are doing wrong, but what *they* are doing right.

The threadbare argument that Japanese workers receive less pay than their American counterparts simply doesn't wash any more. Over 90 percent of Japan's 116 million people now freely admit that they belong to the middle class and can boast of having all the niceties in life that are commensurate with this status. In 1980 salaried workers in Japan earned an average of $25,700 per year, and the average annual income of all Japanese employees was about $17,000.

What brought all this about? The sharp rise in productivity and quality control is almost universally credited to a period in history shortly after World War II when W. Edwards Deming, an American mathematical physicist, was invited to Japan to teach statistical methods to Japanese industry. It is important to bear in mind that the image of Japanese consumer goods at the time was at the lowest point in history. Yet Deming, by working together with a renowned quality control specialist and with Tokyo University professor Kaoru Ishikawa, developed a national program that is credited with reversing the scarred image of Japanese-made products and changing them into sought-after commodities throughout the world.

The nucleus of the plan devised by Deming and his associates centered around the introduction of a management system of statistical techniques, including control charts, process capabilities, and statistical sampling plans, augmented by quality control circles. A quality control circle (or QC circle) is a small group, usually not exceeding 10 employees who do similar work, that voluntarily meets once a week for the purpose of discussing problems related to quality. At these meetings solutions are recommended and, when possible, implemented. The groups are all taught elementary techniques of problem solving, including statistical methods. Typical problems include reducing such things as defects, scrap, rework, and machine downtime.

The quality control principle might seem somewhat overly simplistic until one analyzes the complete ramifications of the process and takes into consideration the Japanese work attitude. The viewpoint of a Japanese worker toward his or her job can best be decribed as one of complete and utter dedication. To remain idle when there is work to be done is a trait seldom observed in Japanese industry. A worker's job in Japan is regarded as something that will provide the worker with the good things in life and should therefore be nurtured with reciprocal care and devotion. The simple act of talking about activities unrelated to the job during working hours is considered to be in extremely bad taste by the Japanese worker.

Japanese managers, to a greater degree than their American counterparts, recognize their workers as an integral part of the organizational structure. They go to considerable lengths, both on and off the job, to make employees feel more secure. Participation of all personnel in job-related and free-time activities is common practice in Japan, with the company sponsoring many family social events. Employees are virtually never discharged from an organization, except under the most unusual circumstances.

The end result of this policy seems to be that Japanese management has succeeded in convincing the worker that he or she will be taken care of at all times without resorting to strikes, grievance procedures, unemployment insurance, and the dozens of other regulatory practices so common in the American industrial complex. The system has worked extremely well in Japan, possibly because the Japanese attitude toward labor–management relations is about 180 degrees removed from the thinking in American industry. Yet even if we concede that importing the Japanese work attitude wholesale to an American factory is impossible, there have been numerous instances where the QC circle and its related methods have worked well in America.

One case involves Westinghouse, where the QC program is called "Volunteers Interested in Perfection" (VIPS). A similar program at Boeing titled "Participative Employee Problem Solving " (PEPS) has been enormously successful. A bolder approach has been successfully used at the Grand Rapids, Michigan, plant of the Japanese-owned Yamaha Musical Products, Incorporated. Productivity at this plant, predictably perhaps, had fallen far below that of its sister plants located in Japan. Management (which is about half American and half Japanese) therefore sent some of its American employees to Japan for a one-to three-month training period. There they were exposed to the customs and traditions of their position by Japanese standards and acquired a better understanding of the Japanese industrial scene. Upon returning to their jobs in Grand Rapids, they were enrolled in a vigorous program of discussion among plant workers designed to create an atmosphere of greater cooperation between labor and management. Since the Yamaha program was first initiated, productivity at the Grand Rapids plant has risen dramatically.

These are, of course, relatively isolated instances. The principles of statistical controls for quality augmented by QC circles, introduced by Deming over 30 years ago, have been slow to catch on in America. In an interview with the editors of *Quality* magazine published in the February and March 1979 issues, Deming pointed out that the principles he brought to Japan in 1948 received little attention in America. "They were well received by engineers," he said, "but management paid no attention to them."

Concerning the future outlook for quality control in America, Deming is similarly unencouraging. He believes that the QC gap between Japan and the United States will widen even further in the years ahead. "Americans depend too much on inspection," he says. "And inspection is unsatisfactory. Even 100 percent inspection using automatic testing machines doesn't guarantee quality. It's too late—the quality is already there." What's needed, according to Deming, "is a nationwide commitment to quality. The Japanese made that commitment nearly 30 years ago and are still learning and moving ahead faster and faster."

All this adds up to the fact that we don't have to learn anything about the principles of quality control from Japan. We invented them. All we have to do now is apply this knowledge. Let's hope that we'll begin to do this before we are hurt too badly to recover.

ORGANIZATION IS MORE THAN JUST A BEAUTIFUL CHART

I have seen many beautifully drawn organization charts. Some were incredibly complex. Some were in living color. Some even contained three-by-five photos of the incumbents to the indicated position. Yet I have never seen an organization chart that ever told me anything.

Organization charts, for the most part, provide an interesting decoration on the wall of the chief executive's office, and little more. Let me hasten to explain that these remarks are directed at organization charts and not organization, which is a vital and necessary part of any well-run business. Unfortunately, however, many company executives refuse to differentiate between the two. Instead they regard the organization chart as something akin to sacred proclamation upon which the firm's entire operational structure must be based for all time to come.

Any organization chart, even one that is accurate and well maintained as far as company personnel is concerned, is essentially a static thing. It represents the chain of command in a company at a given point in time. An organization, on the other hand, is anything but static. It changes pattern day by day, week by week, in response to events, improvements, and business climate. The changes in an organization are brought about by human behavior. Whether or not this human behavior takes the form of a weak general supervisor or a lawmaker who cares little about the firm's general interest is unimportant as far as the chart is concerned. Charts do not reflect these changes. They simply hang majestically on the wall, usually unchanged in structure, with company management serene in the belief that The Organization Chart is the final and ultimate design for the company's operating road map.

The almost universal worship of the organization chart did not come about through mass telepathy between the managers of our nation's leading firms. The practice has been ingrained through many years of management education that attempts to scientifically design an organization structure that would fit any and all business. I submit that this is a throwback to the sales pitch given by the snake-oil sellers of another era, who peddled medicine that was supposed to cure all diseases from leprosy to trench mouth.

Because they are influenced primarily by human factors, good principles of organization cannot be brought about scientifically. Yet many management textbooks have attempted to do this. Graicunas's theory outlines a formula that tells exactly how many people should report to any particular manager. According to Graicunas, no more than five or six people should report to any one person, yet many well-run companies have far more reporting to key executives.

People, together with their capabilities and shortcomings, must always take priority over the bloodless requirements of an organization chart. The relationships should be based on the jobs, the people in the jobs, and the conditions surrounding the jobs. Otherwise we are sacrificing results for rituals.

I know of one case, for example, where it made sense for the chief industrial engineer to report to the controller because the manufacturing vice-president was heavily sales oriented and the works manager was wrapped up in product research. On the other hand, the controller was deeply interested in the management implications of industrial engineering. Principles of organization are admittedly necessary, but they should be kept flexible enough to fit existing conditions. Additional problems concerning organizational responsibilities are often caused by overlapping lines of authority and poorly prepared job descriptions.

In designing job descriptions, particularly for managerial and semisupervisory employees, the best advice is to keep the definitions as broad as possible if they must be made at all. The catchall phrase "and such other duties as the installation head may prescribe" has, I know, been overworked. On rare occasions it might even be abused. However, when compared with the abuses that have occurred because of superspecialization, the damage has been negligible.

If we are ready to accept the premise that good organization must be geared to the people in the job rather than the job itself, the logical question follows: How can a clear and workable standard of performance be developed? The initial step is to prepare the ground for definite responsibility for which management can hold accountable the entire executive or supervisory group. In general, executives understand their main responsibilities, especially if they have written job descriptions.

As an example of an effective way to proceed, let's take the sales manager. His or her primary responsibility is to produce more sales and thereby improve the profit position. From a realistic standpoint it is debatable whether we can hold sales managers responsible for *total* sales, since they do not control things like the weather, changes in buying habits of customers, or quality of service provided by individual plants. They can, however, be held directly responsible for improvement of the selling organization, for concentration of effort by all sales personnel along proper channels, and for obtaining specific performance. They can also be held accountable for total sales budget performance and, to some extent, sales stability.

To arrive at a standard, the president, controller, and individual executives should jointly determine the acceptable range of performance for each standard that will apply. The available data on that standard in terms of industry performance, company performance, and individual performance should also be considered, as well as the influence of differing ranges of performance on a given standard upon sales and profits. With these data, it should not be difficult for everyone concerned to arrive at an agreement on what is necessary to accomplish the results that the company expects in terms of total sales or profitability.

Once standard performance has been attained for one or more positions—and geared to the individuals in the position—the entire organization can be developed into a more workable unit based on individual responsibility and accountability and knit together by clearly delineated lines of authority. The method of accomplishment will vary somewhat depending on the company itself and the people who make it operate. However, here are some principles I have found effective as general guidelines for better organization. I've never seen these rules in any textbook. They have been developed during long years of experience.

1. There should be a policy or "road map" set up before the organization is formed or a reorganization contemplated.

2. There must be a yardstick for measuring accountability.

3. Because there are no scientific rules of human behavior, a scientific approach to the problems of organization will create more problems than solutions.

4. To have employees in certain positions report to a predetermined officer of the company is ridiculous. Workers should report to the *logical* person, to be determined by the job or other conditions. There should be no cut-and-dried rule about who is to report to whom—it all depends on the setup or specific conditions within the company.

5. Organization and its tool the organization chart are only means to an end, not ends in themselves.

6. Top management must realize that any organization is in a continual state of flux. It is subject to change every time personnel or production policies or sales methods are changed.

7. Sound management practice recognizes that any person in an organization can be replaced. Ideally, the chief executive should be able to look at the organization and ask, "Could I fire that employee tomorrow if it were necessary?" If the answer is no, management could be in for big trouble.

8. Good organization cannot exist without 100 percent participation.

9. There is a definite relationship between the size of the company and the necessity for formalized organization.

10. To bring about good organization, one should forget theo-

retical ideals and accept the fact that personnel is the keynote: the employees that are available, or can be made available, to the firm.

Once true organization is achieved, an organization chart might then be in order. If one is drawn up, it might be helpful to prepare it according to the same general principles used by the men who drafted our Constitution. In other words, recognize that it is designed to operate only at this point in time, and as changes occur amendments may be necessary. Otherwise, the charts rather than company management could end up running the organization.

9

Making the Press
Work for You

Humility may get you into heaven, but it'll never
win you a new account or a promotion.

Anonymous

The media, including newspapers, magazines, and TV commentators, often seem to operate on the premise that bad news generates more consumer interest than good news. That is bad news for the business community, which understandably wants to project a favorable image of its products or services.

It is not my intention to dwell at this time on the rights and privileges guaranteed under the First Ameendment or whether or not the excessive coverage of bankruptcies, scandals, product shortcomings or labor–management difficulties should rate the mass coverage normally provided by the fourth estate. What is obvious, however, is that, with the possible exception of the Chrysler Corporation, few firms have their accomplishments publicized as much as their occasional shortcomings.

Right or wrong, this condition has generated an attitude in the business community to keep the company's press coverage confined to expensive paid advertising—even to the extent of stonewalling inquisitive reporters whose published opinions might do a company more harm than good. An example of this involved the Mobile Corporation who, in a fit of ire following publication of an unfavorable news item, pulled its advertising from the *Wall Street Journal* and refused to answer reporters' questions.

Yet, like it or not, our nation's press is a king-sized factor in molding public opinion. That is why many organizations have retained high-priced publicity firms whose chief role is to project a favorable corporate image through well-structured press releases. Unfortunately, they seldom make it past the desk of the business editor's secretary.

From the standpoint of editors and their staff, who must cull through literally reams of unsolicited hype every business day to find one or two features to include in a limited space of column inches, the press cannot be wholly faulted for its apparent lack of enthusiasm. The text of many of these communications unabashedly suggests that the policies of the firm are something akin to an unblemished model for all business that, if emulated by their competitors, would instantly eliminate the national debt, racial discrimination, and acne among teen-agers. Communications of this type are immediately recognized for what is known in the trade as "puff pieces" and summarily consigned to the nearest wastepaper basket.

How then does a firm get a message across to the users of its products or services without resorting to paid advertising that can cost tens of thousands of dollars a printed page and is not as widely read as straight news items?

Let's go back to the Chrysler Corporation, which was in the throes of bankruptcy a few years back and, largely through the efforts of Lee Iacocca (forget for a moment about the huge government bailout that has since been repaid), came to become what is one of the hottest subjects of the American press. I doubt if the board of directors at Chrysler planned it this way, but the secret to the subsequent rash of favorable publicity was that the bad news *preceded* the good news. The press was unmerciful in reporting Chrysler's previous difficulties. Therefore, when it developed that the situation was not as bleak as originally reported, the good news suddenly became news that was fit to print.

About this time I can hear some of my readers saying, "So what do I have to do to get some favorable press coverage? Are you suggesting that I go to Chapter Eleven?" The answer is no! I discovered the magic formula almost 25 years ago when I realized that my own management consulting firm, Patton Consultants, Incorporated, needed some widespread news coverage that could enhance the company image and generate some new clients. The formula I employed was extremely successful for me. With a few modifications, it can be equally successful for anyone with the will and tenacity to place it into effect.

About 25 years ago Patton Consultants had just completed several highly successful wage incentive programs. We had documented proof that the improvements we made had raised the clients' profits and increased take-home pay for the employees. We were understandably proud of the accomplishment, particularly when the chief executive officers of some of these firms were lavish in their praise. Many gave us blanket permission to use the incidents in our promotional program as representative case histories.

I was of the opinion that a brief item in the press would go a long way toward generating additional clients and distributed a press release to several dozen members of the news media. Nothing happened. Subsequent investigation developed the fact that, because the potential news item was frankly conducive to self-interest, the media, which after all is in the business of selling paid advertising refused, understandably perhaps, to print the material as straight news.

The problem was to determine the type of material editors would publish. It would also help if the material could be placed in a medium that catered exclusively to people in lines of endeavor similar to that of the clients we had successfully served. Was there such an outlet? Indeed there was. *Not one, but literally hundreds of them.* In the parlance of journalism, they are called the "trade publications." They are circulated among business people and management entities in various industrial categories that range from heavy construction to the textile industry. All of them are hungry for material that deals with case histories of how a specific company, faced with some typical operational problem, overcame the difficulty and produced a better product or streamlined their operation to achieve lower costs.

I selected *Modern Converter Magazine*, which catered to people in a field where we had considerable experience. In a brief letter I explained our recent accomplishments and offered the story to their readers.

The reply came back that they would indeed be interested if the material were written up in a manner that would comply with the editorial standards of the magazine. Rather than attempt this myself, I consulted a copy of *The Working Press of the Nation* at my local library and queried several professional writers to whom I outlined my project. I settled on a writer named Jack Lewis, who at the time had several hundred magazine credits to his name, many in the field of business and management. The result was a series of articles published in four consecutive issues of *Modern Converter Magazine.*

This was the first of several hundred published articles that were placed by Jack Lewis and me. To say that the program was successful is a gross understatement, since each of the printed articles was used to generate additional business in the following manner. Immediately after publication I arranged with the publishers to supply me with 500 reprints of the published text. These were mailed to top management officials all over the country as an example of Patton Consultants' mode of operation, together with a brief cover letter outlining our organization's expertise in various areas of productivity improvement. These mailings produced a wealth of leads that resulted in numerous new clients. Many of these, in turn, were used to provide more material for more magazine coverage. Thus, we had a self-perpetuating chain of media coverage and new material for our direct mail program. Publications that used this material, in addition to *Modern Converter Magazine*, included *Industrial Engineering, Business Management, Management Review, Production Maga-*

zine, Assembly Engineering, Woodworking & Furniture Digest, Rubber Age, and others too numerous to mention.

In each case the coverage was free, and in some cases we even got *paid* for the article. During the 20-year period we used this program I was able to make the claim that I had more articles on management published than all other consultants combined. The process is so simple that I often wonder why all business executives have not taken advantage of this viable marketing formula. Yet, incredibly enough, if there is anyone who is presently using this sure-fire formula, I have yet to hear about it.

I am sure about this time some of my readers may be mulling over the question, "Why should I tell my competitors the way I work?" Let's meet this question head on. With possibly a few exceptions, a firm has more to lose by being secretive than it has to gain. In my opinion, the old expression, "Macy's doesn't tell Gimbel's," should be permanently put to rest along with a few other depression-era idioms. My philosophy is "If you've got it, flaunt it."

In an era marked by sophisticated market research and instant communication, it won't be long till your competitors know what you are up to anyhow. So why not jump on them and let the world know exactly who it was that innovated this improved product or procedure?

In addition to communicating through the media, I've even found this policy to work in my personal life. Some of my best friends have also been my most vigorous competitors. But communications is a two-way street. I've gained considerable input from these people about their own operations that enabled me, in some instances, to start where someone else had left off.

HOW THE PROGRAM CAN WORK FOR YOU

Despite inevitable frustrations and occasional blunders, there are times when everyone encounters some incident of which they can justifiably feel proud. Ideally, the customer to whom the product was sold will be equally impressed. When this occurs, a personal call on this individual with the request that you would like to write up a case history of the program or situation for possible use in a magazine article will almost always result in an affirmative reply, particularly if you state that using the customer's name will also re-sult in favorable publicity for your client. In some cases where it was deemed mutually beneficial, I've even included the client's name on the by-line of the published article.

Having acquired permission, the next step is to select a possible publisher. An exceptionally strong article with general appeal might make it in one of the mass circulation publications like *Dun's Review, Forbes,* or the *Wall Street Journal.* But don't bet on this. Even though I have successfully placed material in each of these general publica-tions, most of them have their own staff and are deluged with much more material than they are able to use. Your best bet is in the trade publications that cater to a field or occupation in your area of inter-est. With your specialized knowledge, you can present yourself as an authority.

To find out which publications use material related to your own field of endeavor, there is a book on the subject titled *Writer's Mar-ket.* It is available to all bookstores or at your local library and is pub-lished by F&W Publications, 9933 Alliance Road, Cincinnati, Ohio 45242. *Writer's Market* lists literally hundreds of trade, technical, and professional journals, together with addresses, editors' names, sug-gested word length, and other important requirements. For easy reference the publications are even catergorized alphabetically by the respective trade or occupation that they serve. For submissions relative to Advertising and Marketing, for example, my *Writer's Market* lists 15 different publications that use this type of material. Other fields like Automotive, Construction and Contracting, and Electronics have even more magazines from which to choose.

Select a potential publisher from the choices listed. Then either telephone or write a brief letter telling what you propose to submit. Be sure to include facts, figures, and a short explanation of why you feel this material would be well received by the readership. If you get turned down, try another magazine in the same general field. If you get a go-ahead, you are now ready to roll.

WRITING THE ARTICLE

While most of us are fairly adept at writing letters and reports, writ-ing for publication is a specialized art. If you or a member of your organization is particularly good at transferring thoughts to the written word, by all means handle the project yourself. But bear in mind that there are a number of specific rules that must be followed if the material containing your by-line and company blurb is to see the light of day.

1. Don't overglorify your company. Stick to the facts concerning the incident on which you are reporting. There is nothing that waves a red flag in front of an editor more than an unadulterated puff piece disguised as a straight news item. It's all right to cite documented facts concerning the project you're writing about. But don't fall into the trap of opening your article with a statement like "The Acme Grommet Company, manufacturer of the world's best grommets, added another item to its vast inventory of superior products last month when . . . ." This type of chest beating will probably do no more than net you one of those politely worded printed rejection slips.

2. Stay within the magazine's word length requirements. If the editor fails to provide a maximum word length, check a back issue and be guided by a typical article.

3. Write from the viewpoint of the reader. Wherever possible avoid technical terms. Pay particular attention to the "bottom line." If the method, procedure, or improvements you made for a customer or client increased net sales by 24 percent, say so. If costs were reduced by 20 percent as a result of this innovation, tell them about it. This is the type of advice industry people are hungry to acquire. Forget about your competitors' learning this. They probably already know about it.

4. Write in a lively style. Open with a strong, eye-catching lead that promises the reader something in the paragraphs ahead. Then explain step by step exactly what was accomplished. Try to develop a title that "baits" the reader (and the editors) to read on. Some examples I used in my own material include "The Cornwell Success Story," published in *Woodworking and Furniture Digest*; "Wage Incentives Cut Costs, Increase Production at McCrearys," published in *Rubber Age*; "New Loan Criteria for Bankers," published in *Bankers Monthly*; "Don't Worry about Production—Watch Maintenance Costs," published in *Iron Age*.

5. In a separate cover letter, include a brief (150 words or less) thumbnail biography of the person whose name appears on the byline and, although this is optional, a black and white glossy photo of the author.

In the event you feel that no one in your organization has the professional expertise to put the article across in the manner you desire, consider hiring a professional writer to structure the material for you. It may cost a couple of hundred dollars, but the impact of a text professionally written could make the expenditure well worth the cost particularly if your own employees must be removed from regularly assigned duties to accomplish the project.

A comprehensive listing of professional writers is available at your local library in a book titled *The Working Press of the Nation— Freelancer's Directory*. It also may be obtained from the National Research Bureau, Inc., 424 North Third Street, Burlington, Iowa 52601. This book lists thousands of free-lance writers from all areas of the country by name, address, specialty, and publications in which their work has appeared.

In my own case I found that hiring an outside writer was well worth the expenditure. Such a journalistic expert will also know of all potential publishers of your material and their editorial requirements. She or he probably can suggest candidates for future articles and additional exposure.

AFTER THE ARTICLE APPEARS IN PRINT

Once your article is read by thousands of people, some of whom are potential customers, both you and the company you represent may gain some measure of prestige. But having your message piped into our nation's business offices is only the first step. To gain maximum exposure, the next thing you must do is to arrange with the publisher to provide you with reprints of the article. Most publishers are happy to do this for a small cost. If the magazine is not equipped to do this you can, with permission of the publisher, arrange to have this done elsewhere. For a small mailing program, there's always the office copy machine.

These reprints should be mailed, together with a cover letter outlining your firm's product or services, to top management officials who qualify as potential customers. If you don't have the names of these people, you *should*—even if you decide not to implement this program. Firms specializing in mailing lists can furnish you with an updated list of names in virtually any category you request.

If you follow up this procedure with a new feature and a new pitch for a potential customer's business from time to time, I can practically guarantee that the results will exceed your most optimistic estimates and be more effective than countless thousands of dollars of paid advertising. If this sounds like an overstatement, consider the fact that people subscribe to magazines and periodicals to read the *features*. They may give superficial attention to paid advertisements, but I doubt if five people in a hundred read all the ads in their entirety.

HOW DO I GET NEW MATERIAL FOR
AN ONGOING PROGRAM?

When journalists are confronted with this oft-repeated question, they invariably respond by saying, "Ideas are all around you. All you have to do is to look for them." This is true for every line of work or endeavor.

I will freely admit that in the business of management consulting, where my firm was charged with finding industrial irregularities and implementing remedial action, ideas may have been somewhat easier to come by. But I'll unequivocally state that the program outlined here can be adapted for virtually any line of business if it is geared to providing information or advice to potential clients in a specialized field. And it is here that the trade publications offer maximum exposure to readers who are really interested in what you have to say.

The first few articles should come relatively easy, even if your business is not the type that has strong ties with customers or clients. For example, there are always in-house improvements that would be interesting to counterparts in your line of work. On these, of course, you will require no clearance or permission from outside sources. Later, if you find yourself "scratching" for new ideas, here's a dandy trick I learned that can guarantee a steady influx of potential material. Circulate a questionnaire among your key personnel who have daily contact with present customers or who work in areas where research and development are accomplished. In my own case, the questionnaires were distributed to industrial engineers who worked on site with clients. In other lines of endeavor it might be necessary to circulate them among salespeople, marketing people, mechanics, quality control employees, or even assembly line workers.

The questionnaire should be headed by an explanation of the

ongoing program. It should point out that the firm is actively soliciting ideas for articles suitable for magazine publication that point
up new methods, ideas, and concepts that were used by the firm to
benefit the client directly or indirectly.

Actual questions contained in this handout will vary depending on the type of business. In addition to requesting a brief
explanation of the idea, it should contain questions like the following:

1. If the suggestion concerns a client or customer, do you think
   they would be receptive to our publishing this material?
2. Can you suggest a title for the article?
3. If the idea requires permission, please list the names and titles
   of people we can go to for official approval to publish this material.
4. Cite, if you can, actual savings or benefits that were derived
   from the use of this improvement or innovation.
5. Would you be willing to lend your time and effort toward developing an article of this type for publication?
6. Would the material contained in this proposed article be conducive to photographs used in support of the printed text?

The questions should be designed to give you enough information so that a management decision can be reached regarding
whether or not to go ahead. It should then close with a statement to
the effect that, should the idea achieve publication, the suggestor
will receive credit in the text of the presentation and be rewarded
with a stated cash payment.

Following screening of incoming questionnaires, it may then be
necessary for a company executive to confer with the customer or
client for additional information and formal approval. This will be
much easier than you think. Out of several hundred articles I placed
on behalf of Patton Consultants, I have only been turned down
twice. In fact, you can almost always expect to accumulate a wealth
of new and interesting information during this visit. It may well
flesh out your article in ways that will increase its appeal to magazines in your specialized field.

The advantage of an ongoing program of this type is that it
feeds on itself. New clients or customers acquired through the proc-

ess are, of course, potential for future articles. As to getting your workers involved through the questionnaire process, I also found that once an employee finds his or her name in print it appears to stimulate a desire among co-workers to also get into the act.

During this time, in addition to the obvious benefits, I can confidently state that, because of having my name and company appearing favorably in the public eye, there are few management people today who do not recognize the Patton name in conjunction with the consulting field.

Summary

Since this book opened with the analogy of labor, management, and government as the three heads on a three-headed monster, it is perhaps fitting we close on a similar note. I have tried to present the industrial situation today as I see it and to share some of the methods by which I have solved many commonplace problems. Both government and labor, two of the heads on this monster, have been subjected to some strong but well-earned criticism. I have, however, been particularly harsh on management. Many of you have probably bristled at some of the uncomplimentary things I've said about practices that may now be standard procedures in your factories and offices. If you are only mildly disturbed by the things I have said, I am disappointed. Frankly, I hoped to get you so worked up that you would go back to your company and do something about the productivity gap that now poses such a serious threat to our entire economic system. To those readers who may feel that I have spent a disproportionate amount of wordage on the management segment of our economy, permit me to explain why management must assume the greatest portion of the blame.

First, it's important to recognize the fact that both government and labor, no matter how sympathetic toward solving the productivity problem, are both motivated by interests that, if not downright selfish, are at the least personal bread-and-butter issues. Managers, on the other hand, are *being paid* to make sure that the productivity level of their company will be high enough to bring the firm a reasonable return on its investment. But even more important, few would deny that, of the three entities, management is in a vastly better position to initiate remedial action against the numerous shortcomings cited in this book.

If we agree that both government and labor have been apathetic if not downright hostile toward productivity improvement, the logical question follows: What has management been doing while the ship is sinking? Unfortunately, the response of managers for the most part has not been overwhelmingly reassuring.

A poll conducted by Louis Harris a few years back pointed up the fact that nearly half of all executives agree with the widespread premise of organized labor that productivity gains benefit companies at the expense of their workers and that productivity gains are usually contingent on workers being displaced by machines or on employees working much harder. Therefore, with neither side fully committed, productivity improvement can best be compared to a painful therapy for a serious disease that both doctor and patient refuse to fully recognize.

Incredibly enough, there even seems to be some confusion concerning exactly what is meant by "productivity." Without worrying about other people's definitions, I'd like to submit my own simple, logical definition of productivity as it applies to today's industry: the ratio between what is produced and what must be consumed in order to produce it.

Regardless of semantics, the bottom line appears to be that, since neither government nor labor is willing to take any giant steps toward remedying our productivity deficiency, this leaves one, and only one, area in our economy that is equipped to run the ball on this very important issue—*management!*

Management must get enthusiastic and serious concerning the subject of productivity improvement. It must act, not talk! Reversing the present trend won't be easy. It would be helpful if government and labor would cooperate with the king-sized effort that will be required to bring this about. Yet before this can happen management must take the lead. Otherwise all we can hope for is more unrealistic demands by organized labor and more campaign oratory delivered by our nation's politicians in meaningless generalities because specifics concerning productivity improvement might offend a portion of the voting public who might be asked to work a little harder.

I'd like to believe that America is up to the challenge we face in the years ahead. History clearly indicates that we, as a people, have the ability to overcome almost any adversity once we clearly recognize the need to do so. In my lifetime I have seen our country recover and prosper after the worst depression in history. When our naval fleet was shattered at Pearl Harbor, we possessed the will, the dedication, and the fortitude not only to rebuild our devastated war machine, but also to ultimately achieve unconditional victory.

While the nations of Europe were sifting through the rubble created by the giant conflict, I watched American money, equipment, know-how, and ingenuity combine to restore and rebuild the crumbled cities both of our allies and of the defeated countries. Through the magic of television and space technology I have marveled at a close-up look at Saturn's rings and watched men walk on the moon. If all this sounds like flag-waving, I accept the indictment proudly. This country has been good to me. Yet all the things that I currently enjoy were acquired by a system of productive enterprise that now seems to be slowly slipping away.

Our democratic life-style has given us the highest standard of living that the world has ever known. There are few among us who do not cherish our democracy. However, because it is a democracy, we cannot function as many of our authoritarian neighbors do. We cannot *legislate* changes in our approach to increasing our national productivity. We cannot even bring these about—

Unless . . . our federal government gets really interested in doing the job that should be done for the good of the country instead of what is good in terms of winning votes. It must work objectively and cooperatively with both management and labor.

Unless . . . organized labor realizes that continued increases in wages and fringe benefits for its members can come only from increases in productivity. Union leaders must recognize this and convince their membership of the validity of this concept.

Unless . . . both labor and management agree on common goals. Such agreement, incidentally, has been a key factor in Japan's skyrocketing productivity.

Unless . . . managers realize that they have an obligation not only to their stockholders, but to consumers, their employees, and the entire country as well.

Without these actions the three-headed monster is in danger of literally chewing itself up. For our own sake, and that of everyone in this great nation, we cannot permit this to happen.

Index

Y